DRINKING WITH WIZARDS, WARRIORS AND DRAGONS

THEA JAMES, *HUGO AWARD WINNER*

PAMELA WIZNITZER, *MIXOLOGIST*

ILLUSTRATIONS BY TIM FOLEY

CONTENTS

INTRODUCTION

IN 2020, LIKE MANY OTHERS, I had a renewed interest in old hobbies and also discovered a few new ones.

I had always been a home cook, preferring to prepare my meals rather than order in or dine out. Part of this is a holdover from the days when my budget truly could not handle NYC restaurant prices on any kind of regular cadence, but I also learned that I loved making my own meals and took pride in being able to provide healthy, delicious sustenance for myself.

So, in 2020, when everything was closed and we all stayed home to flatten the curve, I wholeheartedly embraced the act of preparing food and carefully planning grocery trips. While the main impetus of this meal prep hobby was the global health crisis, another major driver was having signed a contract to write a cookbook: *Cooking for Wizards, Warriors and Dragons*. In that cookbook, my very first, I had the opportunity to escape work and the world by diving into some of my favorite works of fantasy fiction, reading books, watching films and television shows and playing video games all set in epic worlds where magic is real and heroes and villains vie for victory. These different fantasy worlds were flush with food and drink as well as moments that inspired recipe ideas, so I endeavored to collect as many as I could and bring them into reality.

It was a project that I loved and desperately needed, and I'm so very glad and privileged to have had *CFWWD* as the ultimate pandemic pastime.

One of the sections of that first book was cocktail-focused, and believe me when I tell you it was a lot of fun to write (and taste test). The initial recipe list for *CFWWD* included several cocktails and drinks that didn't make it into the final book because we needed to focus (quite rightly!) on food. So when the opportunity to create a drink-focused follow-up came around, I jumped on it posthaste. In the words of Chris Hemsworth's Thor: "I like it. Another!"

I've been lucky in my professional life to have worked on some fantastic recipe books, including specialty drink and cocktail books, but this is the first time I got to experience the drink-creating side of the process firsthand.

As with my first book, I had the opportunity to reexamine some of my favorite worlds and characters within the fantasy genre and was able to pull together the vision for each recipe. But the real magic-working credit goes to my coauthor. I'm thrilled the amazing, talented, award-winning all-around badass Pamela Wiznitzer agreed to sign on for this journey to Middle-earth and beyond, bringing her creativity, style and exceptional understanding of how to make a damn good drink to this book.

Within these pages you'll find drinks of all sorts, for all types of audiences. As with *CFWWD*, I chose to pull from fantasy novels published by old vanguards of the genre as well as from newer voices. While this is primarily a cocktail book, non-alcoholic options can be found on pg. 7. (Conversely, some of the non-alcoholic beverages share ways in which to impart spirits into the drink to make it alcoholic. Think of this as a choose-your-own-adventure type of hero's journey.)

Some drinks are inspired by potions and others by spells, some are simple wine- or beer-based beverages an intrepid traveler would find in any fantasy world tavern and others are for special occasions, only to be imbibed in courts of high kings and queens of faerie realms (or on New Year's, or Thursday).

Each recipe in this book was a delight to conceptualize, to test, to taste. I hope you'll join me in raising a glass.

Thea James

CONJURING MIXED DRINKS

IT TAKES PATIENCE AND PRACTICE TO CAST A PROPER SPELL.

We've all read stories where young wizards spend years poring over pages of books filled with instructions, insight and history about the magic they wish to master. Even with a valid first attempt, there's a high probability they won't initially unleash the full potential of a spell, but by applying themselves to the craft and taking the time to perfect their techniques, they will eventually obtain the tools and knowledge necessary to conjure the magic.

Dear readers (and wizards), mixology is similar to conjuration, dunamancy or alchemy—there is often so much whimsy and mystery served up in every glass that each sip feels like the result of a powerful incantation. Mixing an enchanting beverage might appear to be a simple task, and yet aspects of the process can befuddle even the most culinarily proficient

individual. Drink-making requires precision, an eye and feel for details, a bit of gastronomic curiosity and a hearty helping of imagination. And while we don't expect you to commit years of your life to studying piles of material to become a tenured headmaster at a school for the mixologically gifted, there are some basic tips (and tricks) to ensure that every stir, shake and pour is a true delight.

Like a bag of holding, this book is chock full of interesting things for you to conjure with a command phrase (or by using the index on pg. 140) but like any magic item, it's a good idea to attune to it before heading into battle. If you're not one for introductions and would prefer to adventure alone, thank you for reading this far. For the rest of you, allow me to be part of your party for the first adventure on your quest to make better drinks.

Cocktails (and all drinks, really) are only as good as the ingredients used to craft them. The recipes in this book contain a wide variety of items ranging from specific teas and citrus juices to esoteric oddities like edible shimmer dust. In nearly every case, fresher is better. It's also good practice to stick with the seasonality of certain foods. For example, I suggest always squeezing your own juices as opposed to purchasing bottled options (as those use a lot of preservatives to make them shelf stable). When it comes to drinking (as with food), better ingredients yield better results. If you are unable to find certain elements of a recipe in your local store, they can be easily accessed online from specialty spice and tea shops.

Remember, drinks are merely catalysts used to create unique and memorable experiences. Feel free to whip up a recipe for yourself or a tray worth at your next party. These pages are filled with cocktails that might seem familiar and others that will be brand new. At their core, they have all been meticulously researched and tested to ensure they evoke the themes, individuals and places of these stories. We hope the charm and enchantment of these tales comes to life with every sip and that for just a moment, you are transfixed by the magic of these drinks.

Non-Alcoholic Substitutions

As part of the creation of this book's recipes, it was important to us both to ensure that wizards, hobbits, trolls, fairy queens and deities of all shapes, sizes and stations could enjoy each of the libations contained herein. That's why the real magic of the recipes we conjured is that all of them can easily be transformed into non-alcoholic versions of their prime iterations.

There are loads of non-alcoholic distillates on the market, so feel free to get creative with your own substitutions, but you can also use the suggestions listed here:

WHITE/CLEAR SPIRITS:
White tea or coconut water

AGED OR DARK SPIRITS:
Over-steeped black tea, which makes the drink more tannic

SPARKLING WINE:
Sparkling grape or apple juice

WINE OR VERMOUTH:
Verjus (comes in a range of styles and flavors)

BEER:
Non-alcoholic beer (your favorite brand from your favorite market)

BITTERS:
Fee Brothers bitters (glycerin-based instead of alcohol-based)

Magical Instruments

Not all wizards use wands to unleash their magic—the end result is the aim, not the tool you use to get there. In other words, you don't need the fanciest bar tools to mix up these drinks. Contrary to popular belief, cocktails can be made almost anywhere if you know how to properly measure your ingredients and are mindful of your shakes and stirs. While How to Set Up Your

Home Bar (pg. 13) outlines the types of tools you will need, here are some at-home hacks that work just as well:

SHAKER: water bottle with lid (with a large mouth for ice), protein shaker, mason jar, quart container and lid

STRAINER: mesh strainer, steel sifter

STIRRING VESSEL: quart container, beaker, beer glass

STIRRING SPOON: chopstick, metal straw

JIGGER: tablespoon (½ oz), ¼ cup (2 oz)

Ice

While often overlooked, ice is the most integral ingredient when constructing a drink. In fact, your mixed beverage should be about one-quarter to one-third water or dilution in order to properly balance the flavors and to allow certain ingredients (mostly the alcohol) to open up and shine. For this reason, it's important that you're mindful of the type and quality of the ice you're using to ensure you don't over- or under-dilute your recipe. Remember the three S's: source, size and surface area.

SOURCE If the source of the ice is the freezer in your house, how clean is that freezer? If that's a question that gives you pause, consider casting *prestidigitation* on your freezer's interior (or just clean it).

SIZE The larger the ice cube, the longer it will take to melt. Certain drinks (mostly stirred) benefit from a larger, slower-melting cube, while other styles (highballs and tiki-style cocktails) are better poured over small cubes or pellet ice.

SURFACE AREA The larger the surface area, the harder it will be to break down and melt. Conversely, the smaller the surface area (or the thinner the ice), the faster it will break down in your drink.

We have created outlines for the average time you should spend shaking or stirring a drink to ensure you're getting the proper amount of dilution. If your ice is smaller or more brittle, reduce the amount of time you shake or stir by a few seconds. If it's larger, increase the time by a few seconds.

Mixological Methods

Combining several ingredients to make a pleasant-tasting potion does not require arcane techniques, but you will find your results are more delicious when you apply the proper method, as outlined in each recipe's instructions.

BUILD Constructing the drink in the glassware in which it will be served. Always build the drink without ice and add ice as the last step to avoid pre-dilution.

STIR Motion of combining and diluting ingredients with ice in a stirring method. This technique is used primarily for drinks that include liquor, syrups and bitters (no citrus, cream, etc.) and to maintain the silky texture of the drink while simultaneously chilling it. Whether you stir clockwise or counterclockwise is up to you.

SHAKE Shaking helps aerate, agitate and activate your drink. The harder you shake in a shorter amount of time, the better your drink will be, while still avoiding over-dilution. Drinks that have multiple ingredients, citrus, creams and whole items like herbs, fruits and vegetables are better shaken. The average shake time should be about seven to 10 seconds. If you are shaking a drink that will be going back over ice (like a highball or a lowball) and topped with carbonation like soda water or tonic, we recommend the "whip shake," which entails quickly moving the drink back and forth in the shaker for no longer than a

> **PRO TIP**
> Place your glassware in the refrigerator or the freezer at least half an hour before making your drinks to have them well chilled in time to serve your beverages.

few seconds without ice, to get the ingredients combined but without excessive dilution. Dry shaking entails shaking without ice.

ROLL The act of moving liquid from one shaker to another by rolling it back and forth to aerate it. This doesn't agitate the drink as intensely as shaking does, and this technique is often used for drinks that have carbonation (like beer shandies) or thick bases (like a Bloody Mary).

FLOAT Taking advantage of the nature of density by layering one ingredient/liquid on top of another. The higher the ABV (alcohol by volume) of a liquid, the better it will lay. Base layers tend to be those with higher sugar content, as those liquids with denser viscosities will naturally sink into the glass. To do this with wine, for example, pour it into the drink over the back of a spoon, which will help disseminate the liquid around the glass instead of in one concentrated area.

INFUSE Saturating, soaking and steeping a liquid with another ingredient or flavor. Infusions are used to create additional layers of structure in a drink. Infusions are mostly shelf stable and can be kept at room temperature, but we suggest keeping them in your refrigerator for freshness.

Glassware

Presentation matters. Lest you forget, we first eat with our eyes—the more enticing the drink, the more enchanting it will taste. While we have suggested glassware and garnishes for each drink, feel free to bring your own flair and finesse when serving your concoctions.

COCKTAIL • COUPE • MARTINI
Used for drinks that are served "up"—without ice—like an aviation or Manhattan.

LOWBALL
Also known as an old fashioned or rocks glass, it holds an average of 8 to 12 ounces of liquid. These tend to be used for shaken cocktails with citrus, such as a margarita, or stirred drinks served over ice, such as old fashioneds or Negronis.

BEER GLASS
The vehicle for drinks with higher volume but can also be used for shandies and Bloody Marys. Usually holds about 16 ounces.

HIGHBALL
A taller, narrower glass typically used for "long" drinks—those with a good deal of non-alcoholic liquid/mixers—such as a paloma or whiskey ginger.

MUG
When serving hot drinks, such as a hot toddy or hot cocoa, these keep your hands safe and retain the temperature of the drink.

HOW TO HOST A FANTASY COCKTAIL PARTY

Put this tome of potent potables and terrific tipples to use by throwing your thirsty loved ones a fantasy-themed get-together to remember (assuming they all make their Constitution saving throws).

Select a Theme

Create an immersive experience by holding to an aesthetic—are you hosting the Yule Ball in time for Christmas? Decking out your home as Rivendell for an upscale Elf soirée or having a few friends over for a boozy elevenses brunch? If you're planning a movie marathon or series bingefest, the theme might be locked in by default. If not, communicate your theme with as much specificity as you can muster. After all, there's a huge difference between the faeries from a Disney movie and those of the Unseelie court.

Create a Cocktail Menu and/or Signature Cocktail

Your drink selection is the liquid embodiment of your theme. How many types of cocktails will you serve? Will you enlist a friend or two to sling drinks with you, or will it just be you and your *invisible servant* (which is to say, just you)? Answering these questions ahead of time will prevent avoidable mishaps down the line. As a general rule, it helps to serve at least one light and refreshing drink and one dark and complex drink. Serving one type of beverage only appeals to guests who share your palate—don't box yourself in. Whenever possible, choose cocktails featuring fresh, in-season fruit. If you'd like a little more to build on, the bibliography on pg. 136 features all the cocktails contained in this book organized by the work that inspired them.

Always Include Non-Alcoholic Options

People love to attend parties. Also, those people may not drink alcohol for reasons that are entirely their own. A gracious host is always prepared and can serve up serious zero-proof cocktail options that look and taste just as delightful as the alcoholic versions you have on offer. Check out our favorite non-alcoholic substitutes on pg. 7 or invest in a few bottles of non-alcoholic spirits like Lyre's Italian Orange, Ritual Zero-Proof Whiskey Alternative or Ghia Non-Alcoholic Apéritif, all of which cost less than $40 a bottle.

TIP: When sending out invites, include an option where guests can indicate whether or not they'll be partaking in the alcoholic offerings so you can better curate your shopping list.

Send (Illuminating) Invitations

Get the word out about your forthcoming adventure at least two weeks before your get-together and use the opportunity to inform your guests about everything they'll need to know. Frame any details, instructions or polite requests according to your theme, e.g., "House robes and wands are encouraged" or "No magical beasts." Resist the urge to keep the theme a secret as part of some surprise reveal and instead make your intentions clear: "*Witcher*-themed cocktail party. BYO swords and an appetite." If you want your guests to dress up, speak not in riddles—tell them to bust out their cosplay best. Inviting folks who are costume averse? Consider snagging a few simple adornments (elf ears, eyepatches, plastic wands or swords) that anyone can use to transform their streetwear into themed attire.

Plan Your Portions and Prep Accordingly

How many hours will your event run? How many guests do you expect, and how many drinks do you expect each guest to down? Keep these questions in mind as you stock your fridge and pantry for the necessary cocktail ingredients to keep attendees pleasantly buzzed throughout your gathering. Running out of the goods in the middle of the party does not a good time make, and no host wants to apparate to the local liquor store in the middle of the festivities. The party needs you, and your future self will thank you for slightly overestimating what you need.

Choose Your ~~Weapon~~, er, Glassware

Step away from the red Solo cups. A martini glass, rocks glass or coupe might not be the first thing your guests notice upon entering your home, but the vessel in which they consume your liquid tribute to fantasy is as important as the theme itself. Treat it as such. Select glassware that best showcases the drinks you plan to serve based on their spirit profile (for a complete breakdown of types, see pg. 9), party theme or both. Search thrift stores, vintage shops and garage sales to find fun, inexpensive pieces so you can build your collection without breaking the bank (or your heart when someone inevitably casts *shatter* on one or two coupes).

Unleash the Hors D'oeuvres

Serving grub with your alcohol is a must, even if a night of Falstaffian revelry is your end goal. A fancy themed party warrants more than mixed nuts. If you're hosting a smaller crowd, creating (or ordering) a charcuterie board artfully packed with meats, fruits and cheeses makes for easy grazing and a tempting centerpiece. But if you've got quite the crowd to please, a cheese board or two won't cover the guests. That's where a build-your-own buffet-style station does the trick: think tacos, sliders, brunch items like waffles, dessert offerings like ice cream sundaes and more. The only prep work for you will be laying everything out, at which point you can sit back and watch your guests assemble their plates themselves, making it a solid win-win. Alternatively, since you're planning themed drinks, compel your guests to provide a few shareable plates of on-brand food instead of bringing a bottle of wine or case of brew.

Make Things Ahead of Time

You can't expect to have a cherry syrup ice ring (see pg. 134) ready to float in your punch if you've popped it into the freezer minutes before your first attendee arrives—only a Time-Turner or white walker could help you there. Whatever you can pull off ahead of time will give you the opportunity to focus on what matters most: spending time with your guests. They will think the party came together as though it were conjured out of thin air. Only you'll know the ancient, behind-

the-scenes sorcery that brought it to life: prior planning. These time-saving tips will go a long way toward that goal.

BATCH YOUR DRINKS

Your home's about to be transformed into a bar, so act like the zealous mixological alchemist you are by prepping various ingredients the night before or a few hours prior to the party. Since you've already received the RSVPs and have an approximate guest list to work with, use that math to help you get sorted. For example, if a recipe calls for 2 ounces of bourbon and you want to serve eight of them, you'll need 16 ounces (2 cups) of whiskey. However, this doesn't take into account how much water a drink will need when it's diluted with ice (whether shaken or stirred), so unless you're already a seasoned bartender, experiment with batching your drinks a day or two in advance to get the hang of it. Save yourself the stress of figuring it out on the fly. Remember: A drink that's slightly too strong is easily fixed with ice and is not something a thirsty friend will pass up. Simple syrups, on the other hand, are freakishly easy to prepare ahead of time—seal them in airtight containers with labels, store them in the fridge to chill and you're good to go.

NOTE: This tip does not apply to citrus, other fresh juices or sparkling drinks like soda, prosecco or beer, all of which ought to be added just prior to serving. Shortcuts and citrus do not mix because oxidized juice tastes like fresh disappointment, and no one wants a flat drink where there ought to be bubbles.

CHILL INGREDIENTS THE NIGHT BEFORE

If you have space, place your gin, tequila, vodka and whiskey in the freezer. DO NOT do this with vermouth or liqueurs, which will freeze.

FREEZE ALL THE ICE

This is best done a day or a few days before the party. Purge your freezer of anything with a smell (which you should do regularly anyway), as any fresh ice you make will absorb lingering odors and flavors. Once you've cleaned out the freezer and made more ice cubes than you've ever seen, place them in zipper-lock bags to keep them fresh. If space is an issue, conjure a cooler. If you're short on time or your ice maker is broken or non-existent, there's always the big ice bin at the grocery store or gas station.

Deck the Hall(s) and Set the Scene

Sure, fairy lights, vine curtains and candles create an Instagram-worthy visual aesthetic, but props like wands, cauldrons, vials and coats of arms ground the scene in a fun interactive way. You can do both, and you likely already own some wizard- or dragon-related items to show off as part of a centerpiece or accent spread. There's no need to break out a snow machine to add a layer of glimmering ice to your Great Hall, though—simple touches can make a big impact, e.g., goody bags packed with single-serving vials of liquid luck. Don't forget to curate a party playlist featuring your favorite series soundtrack—just make sure to preview your music choices beforehand to ensure the selections foster nostalgia ("Never Ending Story") rather than dread ("Swamps of Sadness").

HOW TO SET UP YOUR HOME BAR

Creating your own mixology lair is straightforward enough: A cramped studio apartment isn't going to offer half as many options to set up a working bar as a four-bedroom house with patio. But fear not— what you might lack in square footage can be made up for in creativity and ingenuity.

Need-to-Have Equipment

Do you have enough room to put a medium-size tray on top of a dresser or table? You only need room for:
- a few bottles of liquor
- a shaker
- a mixing glass
- a jigger
- a Hawthorne strainer
- a bar spoon
- a muddler
- a bottle opener

You can get by with improvised tools, of course, but these are relatively inexpensive to acquire and will make crafting cocktails a breeze.

Your options beyond using a tray include but are not limited to:
- a bar cart
- a wall cabinet (even two or three open shelves)
- a sideboard
- a bookcase
- an étagère
- a secretary desk
- a dresser

Nice-to-Have Equipment

Space and budget permitting, the following tools will take your mixology up a notch and make you look like quite the show-off:
- fine mesh strainer
- julep strainer
- tongs
- cocktail picks or skewers
- citrus knife, paring knife or peeler
- cheese knife (frequently found in fancy bar tool sets)
- cutting board
- glass or stainless steel straws
- atomizer
- electric wine opener
- vacuum wine stopper or sealer
- silicone ice molds
- ice bucket and scoop
- ice pick
- wine refrigerator
- specialty cocktail glasses (snifters, cordial glasses, Irish coffee glasses, etc.)
- any tool or accessory made of brass, marble or crystal

Need-to-Have Ingredients

Know the basics when it comes to assembling your drinks.

SPIRITS
- gin
- rum
- tequila
- vodka
- whiskey

LIQUEURS & MIXERS
- vermouth
- orange liqueur
- bitters
- grenadine
- simple syrup
- club soda
- cola
- ginger beer
- tonic water

Nice-to-Have Ingredients
- cocktail olives
- cocktail cherries
- specialty liqueurs

Glassware

To stock up on the right glassware, see pg. 9.

For improvised bar tools you can find at home, see pg. 8.

For non-alcoholic substitutions, see pg. 7.

CALL TO ADVENTURE

Laced with intriguing infusions and unexpected ingredients like kukicha tea, these tipples will cement your status as a drink-slinging hero.

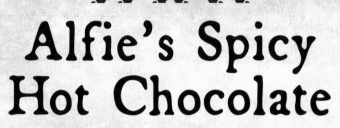

Alfie's Spicy Hot Chocolate

INSPIRED BY MAYA MOTAYNE'S **A FORGERY OF MAGIC** SERIES

Maya Montayne's *A Forgery of Magic* series begins after the death of a crown prince. Prince Alfehr (Alfie, for short) has just inherited his brother's future throne. Desperately clinging to the belief that his brother is still alive, Alfie turns to magic to try to bring him back. First, Alfie scours the palace library, hoping to find answers in older texts. When the answers do not present themselves, Alfie raises the stakes (quite literally) by buying his way into a card game with some of the cream of the crop of San Cristobal's criminal element. The coveted prize: a banned magical book that might just possess some of the answers he seeks.

Of course, things don't go according to Alfie's carefully laid plans. Thwarted by a crafty thief named Finn who can magically change her appearance on a whim, Alfie faces a formidable new obstacle.

Before embarking on his sojourn to San Cristobal's less desirable outskirts and beginning the adventure that will change his life, Alfie spends a good deal of time researching and studying in the library, poring over texts. As crown prince, Alfie is also entitled to servants waiting on his every desire, and his drink of choice is a warm mug of spiced cocoa.

AUTHOR'S NOTE

While it's not recommended to bring a mug of hot cocoa into a library filled with rare texts, exceptions can be made for a concoction this delicious.

INGREDIENTS

- 3 cups milk (or oat milk)
- 2 cinnamon sticks
- 1 Tbsp cocoa powder
- ⅛ tsp cayenne ⅛
- ½ cup dark chocolate chips
- 8 oz honey
- 8 oz rum, whiskey, añejo tequila or cognac, optional
- Grated cinnamon

DIRECTIONS

1. In a pot or warming vessel, add the milk and cinnamon sticks. Simmer on low for 10 minutes (don't let it boil over).

2. Add the cocoa powder and cayenne. Stir to incorporate, then add the chocolate chips and stir to dissolve. Finally, add the honey and stir to dissolve.

3. Once the mixture is heated through, remove from stove and pour into a mug (along with your choice of dark aged spirit, if using). Garnish with grated cinnamon.

Gogu and Jena's Pond Water

JULIET MARILLIER'S **WILDWOOD DANCING**

Juliet Marillier is known for her brand of lush, romantic, folklore-inspired fantasy, and *Wildwood Dancing* is no exception. A retelling of "The Twelve Dancing Princesses" set in medieval Transylvania, the book follows Jena, the second-eldest daughter of a successful merchant. Living in the Piscul Draculi, Jena and her sisters have discovered a magical door that opens the way to the Other Kingdom—a beautiful, joyful fairy realm— each full moon.

For years, the sisters have relished the full moon, sneaking out of their beds, adorned with their gowns and dancing slippers, to waltz the night away outdoors with their fey friends.

The portal to the Other Kingdom, however, is not the only magical facet of Piscul Draculi, as Jena knows. Many years earlier, while Jena and her cousins Costi and Cezar played in the woods surrounding the estate, the three encountered Draguta—the witch of the woods—resulting in Costi's drowning. There's also the matter of Jena's best friend, whom she also discovered in the same woods—a frog named Gogu. Only Jena can hear him, and he is dearest to her heart. (Spoiler alert: Gogu also happens to be Costi.) The pair do everything together, but their favorite adventures are in the woods, with Jena preparing pancakes for two, topped with pondweed and a side of pond water.

> **AUTHOR'S NOTE**
> ....
> Best friends share pancakes.
> And cocktails.

INGREDIENTS

- 1 oz bourbon
- 3 oz English breakfast iced tea
- ½ oz maple syrup
- ¾ oz lemon juice
- 1 lemon wedge
  Gummy frogs

DIRECTIONS

1. Combine first 4 ingredients in a shaker with ice. Shake vigorously for 7 seconds.
2. Strain into a highball glass with ice. Garnish with a lemon wedge and gummy frogs on the rim.

FROM THE BAR

English breakfast tea typically consists of a bold blend of black teas from India, Sri Lanka, Kenya and China.

The Unlikely Queen

INSPIRED BY SARAH BETH DURST'S **THE QUEENS OF RENTHIA** SERIES

There are some fantasy worlds that are generally friendly, in which magic is an aid and a power to always be respected and a force for good. And then there are other worlds that are wholly, utterly lethal. Sarah Beth Durst's *Queens of Renthia* series falls firmly into the latter school of magical thought.

Everything magical in Renthia has the single-minded goal of killing its inhabitants. Fire, ice, water, air, earth— all these primal forces of nature are bent on tearing, rending and eliminating the humans who deign to exist in their reach. Thankfully, there are other forces that can protect the citizens of Renthia from certain death—namely, the protection of their queen, who alone is linked to the wild elemental spirits and can keep

their bloodlust in check. At the outset of *The Queen of Blood*, the first book in the series, an unprecedented attack takes place in the far outskirts of the queendom in which elemental spirits appear to be working together in their assault on humans. Tragically, just about everyone in the village is slain, with the exception of a young girl, Daleina, and her family. As it turns out, Daleina has a rare affinity for controlling the spirits and therefore is an heir to the throne.

Daleina certainly does not care for her call to adventure—she has not trained like other heirs, nor does she possess an easy ability for control. She knows the raw power of these deadly forces firsthand. And yet, despite these disadvantages, Daleina's destiny calls.

INGREDIENTS

- **1 oz peated scotch**
- **1 oz blended scotch**
- **½ oz grenadine**
- **½ oz orange juice**
- **¾ oz lime juice**
- **1 orange peel**

DIRECTIONS

1. Combine first 5 ingredients in a shaker and shake vigorously for 7 seconds.

2. Strain up into a coupe and garnish by flaming an orange peel (expressing the oils over a lit match). Twist and drop the peel into the drink.

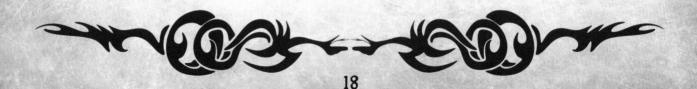

Sting (Like a Hobbit)

INSPIRED BY J.R.R. TOLKIEN'S
THE LORD OF THE RINGS TRILOGY

Bilbo Baggins is a homebody. Or, at least, he was a homebody at the beginning of *The Hobbit, or There and Back Again.* Tricked by the Wizard Gandalf (and due to some of Bilbo's own flustered bumbling), Bilbo finds himself playing host to Thorin Oakenshield and 12 other Dwarves and soon gets swept up into their adventure. Leaving the Shire—and his very well-stocked pantry—Bilbo learns many things on his travels while running into new friends, magical creatures and foes. Along the way, Bilbo also finds some important artifacts: a certain ring (see The Council

of Elrond, pg. 24), but also a troll-hoard of magical weapons, including Sting, an elf-made dagger that serves beautifully as a short sword for a Hobbit and proves particularly effective against giant Mirkwood spiders.

Years later, Bilbo passes Sting to Frodo Baggins (as well as a certain ring), and it aids the young Hobbit on his quest for the soul of Middle-earth. Sting proves powerfully useful, once again, with its ability to detect the presence of Orcs by glowing blue and its ever-sharp edge, capable of cutting through giant spiderwebs that would thwart any other blade.

> **AUTHOR'S NOTE**
> ....
> Like the dagger it is named after, this take on a classic "stinger" may be small, but it's mighty.

INGREDIENTS
- 2 oz brandy
- ¾ oz mint syrup
- 1 mint sprig

DIRECTIONS
1. Combine first 2 ingredients in a shaker with ice and shake vigorously for 7 seconds.
2. Strain into a lowball glass with crushed ice.
3. Garnish with a mint sprig.

A Darker Shade of Red London

INSPIRED BY V.E. SCHWAB'S **SHADES OF MAGIC** SERIES

In the human world, there is just one London. In V.E. Schwab's *Shades of Magic* series, however, there are four different worlds that sit next to each other, and each has a version of London. There's Grey London (aka the regular old Victorian-era human London), in which magic is all but lost and the city is ruled by the twin theocracies of industry and science. There's also White London, a frigid, ruthless and decaying world in which magic is a force to be beaten into submission through relentless domination. The third iteration of the city, Black London, met a fate as dark as its name—it revered magic over all else until it burned, consuming everyone and everything whole.

Then, there's Red London—

the most prosperous and glorious of the four, situated between Grey and White London—where magic is respected and channeled. While this version is located in Arnes (not Britain like its sibling cities), Red London has a river that runs through it: the Isle. Unlike the Thames of Grey London, it is glimmering and magnificent, a red ribbon of light that undulates through the city.

While Red London stands proud, blending magic with technology, seeking balance above all else, there is always the fear that the magic that consumed Black London and its inhabitants may infect its shores. This drink pays homage to Red London's Isle—with the pulsing undercurrent of Black London beneath.

> **AUTHOR'S NOTE**
>
> There are rules that separate the different Londons and dictate how a scant few can travel between each realm. Like its Red and Black London namesakes, this drink also has layers.

INGREDIENTS

- ½ oz cherry-infused rum (pg. 135)
- ½ oz coffee liqueur

DIRECTIONS

1. In a shot glass, add the coffee liqueur, then layer the cherry-infused rum on top (it will float).

Morwen's Chilled Spiced Tea

INSPIRED BY PATRICIA C. WREDE'S *SEARCHING FOR DRAGONS*

The *Enchanted Forest Chronicles* series follows the story of a headstrong (yet always sensible) princess and plenty of dragons, wizards, witches and magicians across four adventures. In *Dealing with Dragons*, Princess Cimorene decides to run away from home and offers herself up to Kazul, King of the Dragons (and notably a female dragon), as a hostage princess. This life, as a chef, librarian and personal attaché, is infinitely more desirable to the sensible Cimorene, who prefers to do good, hard work, than the lack of responsibility and general idleness in the lives of other princesses. Plus, Kazul and Cimorene have a relationship of friendship and respect, which Cimorene hasn't been able to really find in any prince who wants her hand in marriage. All seems to be going well until *Searching for Dragons* when Kazul disappears, and it's up to Cimorene to find her.

At the same time that Kazul disappears, there's also the matter of magic simply disappearing from the Enchanted Forest. King Mendanbar strolls through his magical realm regularly and is finely attuned to the dense threads of magic his kingdom comprises. Imagine his surprise, then, when he comes across dragon scales and swaths of forest completely devoid of magic. Searching for answers, Mendanbar and Cimorene team up with Morwen, a kindly, similarly sensible witch who is friends with Cimorene and lives in Mendanbar's forest. Morwen's abilities are not limited to the magical; she also makes a mean spiced tea, which is always good to soothe the nerves when searching for dragons and stopping annoying wizards.

AUTHOR'S NOTE

The base of Morwen's brew is a spiced tea from trees and flowers from the Enchanted Forest. Spice-infused vermouth is the star of the boozy witch's brew, which can be served at room temperature, chilled or warmed—all at a reasonable lower proof that won't render the drinker insensible.

INGREDIENTS

- 1 (750-ml) **bottle dry vermouth**
- 2 **cinnamon sticks**
- 1 **tsp whole allspice**
- 4 **oz honey**
- 1 **lemon, cut into wheels**
- 1 **orange, cut into wheels**
- 4 **chai tea bags**

DIRECTIONS

1. In a large container, combine the vermouth, cinnamon, allspice, honey, lemon and orange. Stir lightly and let sit for 24 hours. If possible, stir every 4 to 6 hours.
2. Strain to remove the solid ingredients, discard and add the tea bags for 1 hour.
3. Discard the tea bags and pour the liquid back into the vermouth bottle. Note: This mixture will keep in your fridge for up to 6 months.
4. When desired, pour over ice in a lowball glass.

The Divine Wind

INSPIRED BY NAOMI NOVIK'S *HIS MAJESTY'S DRAGON*

Naomi Novik reimagines the Napoleonic Wars with talking dragons in the *Temeraire* series. In *His Majesty's Dragon*, the first book, Captain William Laurence of the *HMS Reliant* captures a French ship and finds a very-near-hatching dragon egg on board. Despite his fervent opposition, the hatchling chooses Laurence as its rider. Laurence names the dragon Temeraire—after a French ship brought into the service of the Crown—and reluctantly accepts his place in the Aerial Corps, where he trades his ship's command for the skies.

Though Temeraire is initially dismissed as a powerless, piddling dragon nowhere near the scale or importance of an acid- or fire-breathing dragon, as it turns out, Temeraire is a Celestial, an exceedingly rare Chinese Imperial breed that possesses a mysterious and coveted ability called the Divine Wind. Using this roar, Temeraire can wreak a great deal of chaos in a number of apolcalyptic scenarios: He can manipulate and destroy elements like wood and stone, call down ships, level towns and summon tsunamis. There's a noticable kick of spice in this drink, so take heed—it's certainly not for the faint of heart.

AUTHOR'S NOTE

This drink's smoked wood chips and Chinese five spice showcase Temeraire's impressive ability while honoring his background as a Celestial dragon.

INGREDIENTS

- 2 oz cognac
- 1 oz Chinese five spice-infused sweet vermouth
- 3 dashes bitters
- Wood chips

TOOLS

Smoking gun and decanter

DIRECTIONS

1. Combine the cognac, sweet vermouth and bitters in a stirring vessel and stir.
2. Prepare the smoked decanter by placing the nozzle of the smoking gun into a decanter and lighting the wood chips on fire to fill the decanter with smoke. Pour the cocktail into the smoke-filled decanter, then seal it.
3. Swirl the cocktail for 15 seconds before pouring into a coupe to serve.

Ellcrys

INSPIRED BY TERRY BROOKS'S **THE SWORD OF SHANNARA** SERIES

Terry Brooks's post-apocalyptic *The Sword of Shannara Trilogy* occurs after a nuclear apocalypse, which might seem more like a science fiction setting than one fit for fantasy, but Brooks's world is one that features Faerie, Elves, Dwarves, Gnomes, Trolls and the like. In the second book of the series, *The Elfstones of Shannara*, readers learn about the Age of Faerie that preceded the birth of man and the Elves who fought against evil and created a magical tree, Ellcrys, to maintain the spell to imprison Demons (the Forbidding).

Ellcrys's fate is intrinsically tied to the overall fate of the world. Though Elves diminished much of their magic to create Ellcrys, they know and remember her importance, guarding her against external forces and through the proliferation of humankind. Ellcrys herself chooses her Elf protectors (the Chosen) to keep her strong and safe as she maintains the barrier to keep the world secure.

There have been three different Ellcrys trees over the course of the series, and each was originally an Elf woman. While most of the Chosen are men, there have been periods of time when Ellcrys picks female Chosen— these women are potential heirs, only selected when Ellcrys believes her life to be in peril.

AUTHOR'S NOTE

A key component in several cocktails, tonic water gets its bitterness from quinine–which is derived from the bark of the cinchona tree. Since it might be hard to derive a tonic from Ellcrys, cinchona is a worthy substitute.

INGREDIENTS

- ½ oz maple syrup
- 3 oz kukicha tea (**twig tea**)
- 3 oz tonic water
- 1 lemon peel

DIRECTIONS

1. In a wine glass, add the maple syrup, then the tea. Stir to dissolve the syrup.
2. Top with tonic water and add ice.
3. Garnish by expressing a lemon peel over the top and placing it into the drink.

The Council of Elrond

INSPIRED BY J.R.R. TOLKIEN'S *THE FELLOWSHIP OF THE RING*

There is arguably no more bittersweet call to adventure than Frodo's in *The Fellowship of the Ring*. While no one seems to think very much of Hobbits—not Men, Elves, Dwarves nor even Sauron himself—Gandalf the Grey knows and values their generous natures and courage. For many years, Gandalf has befriended the Hobbits of the Shire and is responsible for many a Hobbit leaving home for adventure. When Gandalf witnesses his dear old friend Bilbo Baggins perform a remarkable magic trick—slipping a ring on his finger and disappearing before the entire Shire—Gandalf suspects that Bilbo's ring is in fact the One Ring. Encouraging Bilbo to leave the ring behind for his heir, Frodo, Gandalf also encourages Frodo to keep the ring secret and safe—at least until Gandalf can learn more. A truly selfless creature, Frodo agrees and follows Gandalf's instructions, eventually leaving the Shire for Rivendell in secret, following in Bilbo's footsteps and bearing the mysterious ring.

Along the way, Frodo is hunted by the Nazgûl—and pierced in the shoulder by the Witch King's dark blade—luckily, with the help of some new friends, he makes it to Rivendell in time to save his life, though the wound will be with Frodo forevermore, physically and spiritually.

While Frodo doesn't realize it, and certainly never planned for it, much is going on in Rivendell when he arrives. Elrond, Lord of Rivendell, had not sent out summons to form a council, but fate intervened: Boromir had arrived to tell tale of the shared dream he and brother Faramir had and the attack that Sauron's forces levied against Gondor. Glóin, Gimli's father, had received messengers promising the old rings of power to the Lonely Mountain should they know of Bilbo's whereabouts. Legolas brought the news Gollum had escaped his prison and disappeared. With this auspicious group of the three free races of Middle-earth, Elrond called his secret council, to which Gandalf and Frodo were also a party. Sharing the news that Frodo's ring in fact is the One Ring, the council begins squabbling over what should happen to the ring and who should be allowed to use it...until Frodo uses his small voice to speak up. Though he has no desire for adventure, or for the responsibility of bearing the One Ring, Frodo knows he must be the one who takes the ring to Mordor and rids Middle-earth of its corruption.

> ### AUTHOR'S NOTE
> The "call to adventure" in a classic hero's journey is often one the hero refuses and only reluctantly heeds. This drink is as bittersweet as Frodo's decision to take on the heaviest of all burdens for a higher calling.

INGREDIENTS

- 1 oz Campari
- 1 oz grapefruit juice
- 1½ oz white port
- ½ oz lemon
- ¾ oz honey syrup
- Half a grapefruit wheel

DIRECTIONS

1. Combine first 5 ingredients in a shaker and shake vigorously for 7 seconds.
2. Strain the drink into a highball glass with fresh ice.
3. Garnish with a half a grapefruit wheel in the glass.

FROM THE BAR

Developed by Gaspare Campari in the mid-19th century, Campari is a bright red, bitter Italian aperitif that features prominently in the Negroni, boulevardier, Americano and jungle bird cocktails, among others.

The Mimic

INSPIRED BY WIZARDS OF THE COAST'S **DUNGEONS & DRAGONS**

Of all the monstrosities that can be thrown at a party during a Dungeons & Dragons campaign, a mimic is always a solid choice that can tempt and frustrate players to no end. A mimic takes on the appearance of a regular, mundane object—a fancy chair, a tavern table, a bed that looks perfect for a well-deserved long rest—tricking adventurers into thinking they are safe...until they find themselves grappled, bitten and bludgeoned by the mimic's pseudopod attack. Given that these amorphous monsters can perfectly shapechange (or polymorph, in D&D parlance), the cruelest Dungeon Masters will plant a mimic after a battle as an innocuous treasure chest. A mimic's, well,

AUTHOR'S NOTE

For the record, the author has never met one of these fabled "good" mimics in a D&D campaign. If you share that sentiment, this cocktail's for you.

mimicry is so convincing that a twisted DM might let a unlucky player go so far as to open the chest and reach in to grab gold/treasure/jewels before letting the mimic go to town on them.

Technically, per *Advanced Dungeons & Dragons, 1st Edition*, there are two types of mimics. One is generally good and helpful, offering adventurers useful things like food. The other is the one most players are most familiar with—that is, the obnoxious sort that tries to kill you.

This drink is one of the good ones— it will blend in with all the other boozy beverages but is actually a mocktail that seeks to sate, rather than stupify, its imbiber.

INGREDIENTS

- 2 oz pineapple juice
- ¾ oz lime juice
- 1 oz coconut water
- 3 oz tonic water
- 1 pineapple wedge
  Toasted coconut

DIRECTIONS

1. Combine the first 3 ingredients in a shaker with ice. Shake vigorously for 7 seconds.
2. Strain into a wine glass. Top with tonic water, then add ice.
3. Garnish with a pineapple wedge and a sprinkle of toasted coconut.

FROM THE BAR

If you would like to include alcohol in this beverage, we recommend adding 2 oz white rum, vodka or mezcal in Step 1.

The Dreamblood

INSPIRED BY N. K. JEMISIN'S **THE DREAMBLOOD** DUOLOGY

In Gujaareh, a city-state loosely modeled after the great cities of ancient Egypt (but wholly separate and fantastical), there is a class of peacekeepers called Gatherers. Sworn into service for the goddess Hananja, they are charged with collecting dream humors, the most important and powerful of which is dreamblood. As Gujaareh's main magical element, dreamblood is harvested by Gatherers from those who are dying or judged as corrupt by the Hanajan temple's religious order. The person whose dreamblood is harvested dies, but their souls are sent to Ina-Karekh for eternal life. Dreamblood is powerful currency, used by Sharers who redistribute the magic to heal and to help, and it fuels the Gujaareh economy.

Ehiru, one of the most celebrated Gatherers, begins *The Killing Moon* by harvesting dreamblood from an elderly man, who consents and slips peacefully into his last forever sleep. But Ehiru's next visit, to a foreigner who does not observe Gujaareh's customs and does not consent to being killed in the name of a goddess for a sham of eternal afterlife, does not go as peacefully or as smoothly. As Ehiru learns more about the corruption that underlies Gujaareh—he witnesses murders in the name of the dream-goddess, and especially through his lens as mentor to Nijiri, a new Gatherer—Ehiru begins to question everything he has ever believed about his faith and his city.

AUTHOR'S NOTE

While there are ethical questions aplenty in Gujaareh around the harvesting of dreamblood, there is nothing morally ambiguous about harvesting the ingredients for this dreamblood-inspired cocktail. Fresh cherries are always preferred if they are in season, but frozen ones are equally delicious.

INGREDIENTS

- ¾ oz cherry syrup
- 6 oz soda water or sparkling wine
- 1 cherry
- 1 lime wedge

DIRECTIONS

1. Build the cocktail in a highball glass without ice.
2. Stir lightly to dissolve the syrup, then add ice.
3. Garnish with a cherry and lime wedge.

The Hand of the King

INSPIRED BY GEORGE R. R. MARTIN'S
A SONG OF ICE AND FIRE

In Westeros, the highest position of power is the person who controls the Iron Throne. One might think that is the king (also known as the King of the Andals, the Rhoynar and the First Men and Lord of the Seven Kingdoms). However, the king does not necessarily control the Iron Throne (despite sitting upon it)—often, it is the members of the small council who hold the real power in Westeros. While the small council appointees are named by the king and serve at his pleasure, at least in theory, there are political consequences for appointing or dismissing members. Of that small council, comprising seven different positions: Master of Coin, Master of Whisperers, Master of Laws, Master of Ships, Lord Commander of the Kingsguard, Grand Maester and, of course, the Hand of the King. While all of these positions have power, it is the Hand of the King that sits closest to the king—the person in this role possesses the ability to serve as the king's proxy, and most trusted advisor.

The problem, of course, is that the Hand of the king's power comes at a cost—a target on that person's back and a potentially short life expectancy. Certainly that's true for Eddard "Ned" Stark, summoned as the Hand of the King by his friend and king, Robert Baratheon, setting into action a number of terrible events that culminate in Ned's death and the Clash of Kings.

> **AUTHOR'S NOTE**
>
> Ned's time served as Robert Baratheon's King's Hand was very short, but still a better track record than the five men who served as Aerys II Targaryen's Hand.

INGREDIENTS
- 1¾ oz white rum
- ¼ oz crème de violette
- ¾ oz lime juice
- ½ oz simple syrup
- 1 oz tonic water

DIRECTIONS
1. Combine the first 4 ingredients in a shaker with ice.
2. Shake vigorously for 7 seconds and strain into a wine glass.
3. Add the tonic water, then fill with ice. No garnish, as it gets in the king's way when he sips this drink.

The Five Points

INSPIRED BY V.E. SCHWAB'S **SHADES OF MAGIC** SERIES

There are cities that truly possess magic. Not just magic in the fantastical sense, but also in the mundane real world. There have been countless stories, songs and poems written about cities such as New York, Paris or Hong Kong, inspiring generations of artists and writers. In V.E. Schwab's *Shades of Magic* series, London is one such city—one that exists in the regular world as well as in magical parallel worlds. While Red London might be the most prosperous (see A Darker Shade of Red London, pg. 20), White London the most bleak and Black London the most dangerous, Grey London possesses a kind of magic to which most non-magical mortals can relate, including a man named Ned Tuttle. He knows there are worlds beyond the one he sees and lives in every day and yearns for a bit of

that magic. Ned is the proprietor of the Five Points (the tavern formerly known as the Stone's Throw), and like any good proprietor, pays close attention to his clientele. So, when his regulars tell him that Kell Maresh—a lanky, auburn-haired man with heterochromia (different colored eyes)—can bring people magical items from different places, Ned takes notice and sidles up to Kell in hopes of scoring a little magic of his own.

While Ned might not possess the ability to work magic, he does recognize and appreciate magic in its different forms, including the magic of the city of Grey London, notably in the dark hours right as the early golden dawn threads the sky. This cocktail pays homage to the magic of London and Ned's tavern in that layered window of time between last call and first light.

> ### AUTHOR'S NOTE
>
> The Pimm's Cup actually has its roots as a health tonic from mid-19th century London, making this layered variation the perfect choice to encompass all the shades of magic in the various interconnected Londons.

INGREDIENTS

- 1 oz strawberry-infused gin
- 2½ oz lemonade
- 1 oz Pimm's
- 1 oz soda water
- ½ strawberry
- 1 mint sprig

DIRECTIONS

1. Combine the first 3 ingredients in a shaker with ice. Shake lightly for 5 seconds and strain into a highball glass.
2. Add soda water, then ice.
3. Garnish with half a strawberry on the rim and a mint sprig.

FROM THE BAR

An English gin-based liqueur, Pimm's was developed in the early 19th century by James Pimm, the owner of an oyster bar in London who offered it to patrons as a digestive.

The Three Oaths

INSPIRED BY ROBERT JORDAN'S **THE WHEEL OF TIME**

Many ages before the events of *The Eye of the World*, in the Age of Legends, there were men and women who composed the ranks of the magical order known as the Aes Sedai. These "servants of all" (the translation of "Aes Sedai") were gifted with the ability to channel the One Power: the power radiating from the very essence that turns the Wheel of Time. When the Dragon Lews Therin Telamon and the male Aes Sedai failed to end the Dark One and cage him for eternity, the One Power became corrupted and drove all male Aes Sedai to madness, leading to the utter collapse of society and the Breaking of the World.

As is common in epic fantasy, after the world is broken and all seems lost, somehow the world figures out a way to piece itself back together. In the Third Age, the Aes Sedai banded together again as servants of the realm and wary peacekeepers—this time, their ranks comprised entirely of women, as men could no longer be trusted to channel the One Power. Each member who serves as an Aes Sedai is bound to Three Oaths: to never lie, to never make a weapon that could kill another person and to never use the One Power as a weapon unless it is in defense of life. These Three Oaths, firmly solidified in the Third Age, are the heart and soul of an Aes Sedai and the key to their agelessness and power.

> **AUTHOR'S NOTE**
>
> This three-ingredient drink packs a wallop, as do the Aes Sedai who swear by them.

INGREDIENTS

- 1 oz gin
- 1 oz yellow chartreuse
- 1 oz lemon juice
- 1 lemon wheel

DIRECTIONS

1. Combine the first 3 ingredients in a shaker with ice. Shake vigorously for 7 seconds and strain up into a coupe.
2. Top with a lemon wheel.

Fillory and Further

INSPIRED BY LEV GROSSMAN'S **THE MAGICIANS** SERIES

In Lev Grossman's *The Magicians* series, a young man named Quentin Coldwater discovers the magic he has read about in books is actually real. As a child, Quentin cherished a series of books called *Fillory and Further*, chronicling five siblings who find a portal to a fantastical realm and their adventures therein. Many years later as a young man interviewing for university, Quentin snags a spot in Brakebills University for Magical Pedagogy. Here, he learns many things, makes new friends (and lovers, and enemies), tampers with forces beyond his ken and eventually graduates.

Along the way, Quentin also comes to find that the events in the *Fillory and Further* books are fact—the Chatwin siblings did actually locate the realm of Fillory and were its kings and queens. As trained magicians in their own right, Quentin and his fellow Brakebills alumni decide to embark on the adventure of a lifetime: to travel into Fillory and take their thrones. While *Fillory and Further* makes out magic to be somewhat idealized, the real Fillory has very sharp teeth—and the Chatwins are hardly the kindly, brave children of the novels. This drink pays homage to Quentin's call to adventure and the dangers he and his friends face.

AUTHOR'S NOTE

Children's stories can be crueler and more sadistic than their adult counterparts. *Fillory and Further* is no exception, though this cocktail's crisp flavors are anything but harsh.

INGREDIENTS

- 1½ oz pineapple juice
- 1 oz lime juice
- ¾ oz grenadine
- 1½ oz butterfly pea flower iced tea
- 1 lime wedge
- 1 pineapple wedge

DIRECTIONS

1. In a shaker, combine the pineapple and lime juices with ice and lightly shake for 5 seconds.
2. Hold the mixture while building this cocktail in a highball glass—the drink should have three distinct layers. Pour the grenadine into the highball glass and then fill the glass to the top with ice.
3. Carefully and slowly pour the pineapple and lime juice into the glass to form another layer.
4. Finally, to create the uppermost layer, carefully and slowly pour the tea into the glass.
5. Garnish with a lime wedge and a pineapple wedge. Mix before drinking to watch the magic of the color changing before your eyes.

HEROES
&
VILLAINS

Whether shaken or stirred,
don't be surprised if these potent
potables have you questioning
your allegiances by the last sip.

The Last Horcrux

INSPIRED BY J.K. ROWLING'S
HARRY POTTER AND THE DEATHLY HALLOWS

In the sixth book of the *Harry Potter* series, *The Half-Blood Prince*, Harry learns the truth of Lord Voldemort's near-immortality and how Harry was able to survive as an infant even after the Killing Curse meant for him rebounded to its caster. The answer, discovered in a deeply buried memory, is Horcruxes. Using important objects, Tom Riddle, aka Lord Voldemort (see Voldemalört, pg. 49) hid fragments of his soul in order to cheat death. By creating a Horcrux and putting a piece of his soul into such an object, Voldemort ensured he would be tethered to life even if his body was fatally wounded. As long as one Horcrux remained, Voldemort would survive.

While most other Dark wizards would stop at tearing their soul in half to create a single Horcrux, Voldemort saw the value in creating multiple hedges. He split his soul into seven pieces: six into separate Horcruxes and one to remain in his human body. Using items of power from the founding members of Hogwarts (Rowena Ravenclaw's diadem, Helga Hufflepuff's cup, Salazar Slytherin's locket) and items that held powerful significance to Tom Riddle (his school diary, his grandfather Marvolo Gaunt's ring, his faithful snake-kick Nagini), Voldemort created his road map to immortality.

What Voldemort did not count on, however, was his last Horcrux: Harry. When his Killing Curse rebounded, a piece of soul within Voldemort's body attached to the living creature in his midst—a 1-year-old child. In the final book of the series, *Harry Potter and the Deathly Hallows*, Harry learns he is the last Horcrux Voldemort never intended to create– and that he must die in order to stop Voldemort for good.

> **AUTHOR'S NOTE**
>
> This drink's hidden brandied cherry is a play on the unknown, buried Horcrux. Disguised by the black tea-infused rye and dark amaro, this cocktail has hidden depths.

INGREDIENTS
- 2 oz black tea-infused rye
- 1 oz Averna
- 3 dashes bitters
- 1 brandied cherry or gummy worm (sunk to the bottom)

DIRECTIONS
1. In a stirring vessel, combine the first 3 ingredients and add ice.
2. Stir for 10 to 15 seconds until chilled.
3. Strain up into a coupe and garnish with a brandied cherry or gummy worm.

Dracarys

INSPIRED BY GEORGE R.R. MARTIN'S **FIRE & BLOOD**

George R.R. Martin's fantasy continent of Westeros is home to much of the action in his two blockbuster hits: *A Song of Ice and Fire* (which became the television show *Game of Thrones*) and the more recent *Fire & Blood* (which the TV show *House of the Dragon* is based on). Both storylines feature the political machinations, bloody wars and conquests surrounding the Iron Throne, and the noble families that vie to sit upon it. For much of Westeros's history, its rulers hail from House Targaryen of Dragonstone—the dynasty of dragonriders who conquered the Seven Kingdoms and built King's Landing.

House Targaryen's ability to hold on to their power for generations following Aegon's Conquest is largely because of their clutch of dragons—the only surviving family after the Doom of Valyria. By possessing the only dragons left in the known world, the Targaryens had an advantage over the other Westerosi rulers and pressed it for centuries. "Dracarys," the High Valyrian word for dragonfire—and the command given to a dragon to unleash its fire—is a powerful weapon in a ruler's arsenal, one that Daenerys Targaryen gives with confidence and soul-chilling rage in *Game of Thrones* to excellent effect. It's also a command given by her ancestor, Rhaenyra, 150 years or so earlier in the great civil war known as the Dance of the Dragons (see pg. 72). As to whether or not Daenerys, Rhaenyra and the entire Targaryen line fall on the "heroes" or "villains" side of the spectrum, well, that's for the reader to decide.

AUTHOR'S NOTE

Quite fittingly, this drink has a powerful kick—lean into the burn, and imagine torching enemies for a good time.

INGREDIENTS

- 2 oz tequila
- ¾ oz jalapeño syrup
- ¾ oz lime juice
- 3 dashes or drops absinthe
- 1 slice jalapeño

DIRECTIONS

1. Combine the first 4 ingredients in a shaker with ice.
2. Shake vigorously for 7 seconds and strain into a lowball glass with fresh ice.
3. Garnish with a slice of jalapeño.

The Endless

INSPIRED BY NEIL GAIMAN'S **THE SANDMAN**

Neil Gaiman's *Sandman* series should need little introduction. Hailed as one of the greatest comic books of all time, *The Sandman* follows the King of Dreams, Morpheus. At the outset of the first volume, *Preludes & Nocturnes*, Dream is captured by a group of power-hungry humans in an occult ritual gone semi-wrong (the occultists meant to capture Death, but settle for her brother). For 70 years, Morpheus is held in a prison by his captors, which wreaks all kinds of havoc in the world. Without the master of dreams to rule his kingdom, Morpheus's dreams and nightmares escape his realm (the Dreaming) and enter the human world; people everywhere begin to fall into a slumber from which they cannot wake; others use Morpheus's tools, a helm, a bag of sand and a large ruby, to their own aims in ways that further the disastrous impact of Dream's imprisonment.

At its heart, *The Sandman* is a story about stories—sometimes horror stories, sometimes adventures, sometimes with Morpheus as a main character and other times with him as a vessel or a bridge into other tales. Morpheus may be the King of Dreams and the eponymous Sandman, but many of the stories within this series touch on his family, the Endless. The seven children of Night and Time, the Endless form a family of anthropomorphic gods, each representing a different essential force or concept.

Each of the siblings is represented with a different cocktail, using the same core ingredients (gin, citrus and a mixer) and prepared in the same style. They are presented in order of age on the opposite page.

DESTINY

The oldest sibling, Destiny presides over the Garden of Forking ways—a maze—and bears a book as his sigil.

INGREDIENTS

- 2 oz gin
- ½ oz lime juice
- 4 oz ginger beer

Garnish: *1 lime wedge or piece of candied ginger*

DEATH

Dream's favorite sibling, who presides over the last great adventure. She bears an ankh as her sigil.

INGREDIENTS

- 2 oz gin
- ½ oz lemon juice
- 4 oz lemonade or sparkling lemon soda

Garnish: *1 lemon wedge*

DREAM

The third eldest of the Endless and the King of Dreams. Presiding over his realm, the Dreaming, Morpheus bears a helm as his sigil.

INGREDIENTS

- 2 oz gin
- ½ oz lime juice
- 4 oz soda or seltzer

Garnish: *1 lime wedge*

DESTRUCTION

A wise man who presided over The Fulcrum, Destruction was the metaphorical glue that held the Endless together and acted as the family's big brother. Seeing that humankind was turning toward science and unimaginable methods of creation and destruction and wanting no part of it, Destruction chose to walk away from his post and sealed off his realm, leaving his sigil—a sword—behind.

INGREDIENTS

- 2 oz gin
- ½ oz lemon juice
- 4 oz chilled Earl Grey tea
- ½ oz simple syrup, optional

Garnish: *1 lemon wheel or wedge*

DESIRE

One of the two twins in the family, Desire is nonbinary and hedonistic—they preside over their realm, the Threshold (built in Desire's self-image) and use a glass heart as their sigil.

INGREDIENTS

- 2 oz gin
- ½ oz lime juice
- 4 oz grapefruit juice

Garnish: *Salt rim*

DESPAIR

Desire's ever-so-slightly younger twin, she oversees the Gray Realm—a place of smoke and mirrors—and uses a hooked ring as her sigil.

INGREDIENTS

- 2 oz gin
- ½ oz lime juice
- 4 oz coconut water

Garnish: *1 lime wedge*

DELIRIUM

The youngest of the siblings, Delirium was born as Delight, but then changed herself. A chaotic entity of self-realization and madness, Delirium's realm is as ever-changing as its keeper. Her sigil, when she was Delight, was a flower.

INGREDIENTS

- 2 oz gin
- ½ oz lime juice
- 4 oz tonic

Garnish: *1 lime wedge*

DIRECTIONS FOR ALL SEVEN RECIPES

Build the ingredients in a highball glass without ice. Add ice and stir lightly to incorporate. Add garnish before serving.

Gogmagog

INSPIRED BY STEPHEN KING'S *FAIRY TALE*

Though he's best known for his writing as a horror author, Stephen King is no stranger to fantasy fiction—or a big bad villain. In the *Dark Tower* series, for example, King gives his take on Tolkien by writing about a fellowship of gunslingers who travel to the ends of the universe to stop the Tower from falling, thwarting the Man in Black (Randall Flagg/Marten Broadcloak/Walter Padick/and many other names) and the Crimson King. In *The Eyes of the Dragon*, King sets his story in the universe of the Dark Tower (the In-World realm of Delain), in which a plotting magician (Flagg again) seeks to tear down the kingdom. In *Fairy Tale*, King returns once again to fantasy with a classic fish-out-of-water tale: A teenager named Charlie

discovers a portal to another world, called Empis, and explores the strange and wondrous things therein.

Of course, said fantasy world is threatened by an extreme evil called Gogmagog—a giant, Lovecraftian, eldritch horror that lives at the bottom of a very deep well and threatens everything in Empis, as well as the world Charlie calls home. Like so many other fantasy worlds before it, Empis is on the precipice of disaster: When her two moons collide, the Deep Well containing Gogmagog will release its prisoner, and it is up to Charlie and his new friends to try to stop the great and terrible foe from awakening.

This peat-forward drink is as powerful and potent as its namesake. Enjoy at your own peril.

AUTHOR'S NOTE

A word to the wise: there is a great deal of power in names.

INGREDIENTS

- 2 oz peated scotch
- ¾ oz Benedictine
- 3 dashes or drops of bitters
- 1 orange twist

DIRECTIONS

1. In a stirring vessel, combine the first 3 ingredients and add ice. Stir for 10 to 15 seconds until chilled.
2. Strain up into a coupe and garnish with an orange twist.

The Coulter

INSPIRED BY PHILIP PULLMAN'S **HIS DARK MATERIALS**

Philip Pullman's *His Dark Materials* series has its share of larger-than-life characters, including virtuous heroes, some clearly sadistic villains and all of the shades of gray in between. Lyra Belacqua, the heroine, has always thought of herself as an orphan. As a young girl, Lyra was led to believe her noble parents died in an airship accident, and her only living remaining family is her uncle, the charismatic, rich, famous explorer and scholar, Lord Asriel. Raised at Jordan College at Oxford, Lyra's young life is full of rooftop shenanigans and explorations with her best friend Roger, dodging her teachers and yearning for the day she can go on adventures with her uncle.

Then, everything changes. Children from the Jordan College area, and even Lyra's best friend Roger, disappear. They have been taken by the gobblers who have been stealing children and using them for unknown ends. Then, Lyra is told she is being taken to live with Marisa Coulter—a beautiful scholar who works for the Church and who seems to have been very taken with Lyra. Little does Lyra know that Mrs. Coulter is actually her mother (or that Lord Asriel is her father)—though quickly, Lyra learns that Mrs. Coulter's cool confidence and polish hides a sharp, ruthless streak. Mrs. Coulter and her golden monkey daemon are the epitome of confidence and glamor, inspiring trust in all those who meet her, at least at first.

But Mrs. Coulter is anything but trustworthy and is utterly lacking in empathy or compassion. Ultimately, this very posh, powerful woman will do whatever she must to achieve her ends—i.e. kidnapping and experimenting on children (and their souls) in the name of power and religion.

> **AUTHOR'S NOTE**
> Like its namesake, this drink is quite beautiful—but reader, beware: There's always a catch.

INGREDIENTS

- 1½ oz Suze or other gentian liqueur
- 1½ oz safflower tea
- 3 oz sparkling wine, chilled
- 1 lemon peel

DIRECTIONS

1. Add the liqueur and tea into a stirring vessel with ice.
2. Stir for 10 seconds to chill and pour into a flute.
3. Top with sparkling wine. Express a lemon peel over the top and then add the peel to the drink.

The Dragon Reborn

INSPIRED BY ROBERT JORDAN'S *THE WHEEL OF TIME*

In the canon of epic fantasy fiction, Robert Jordan's crowning achievement is the *Wheel of Time* series. Written over a period of more than two decades and finished posthumously by Brandon Sanderson, working from Jordan's outlines, *The Wheel of Time* follows the struggle of light against dark. The adventure begins with a group of young heroes who will become major players in the fight to come. Moiraine, one of the Aes Sedai, driven by the belief she will find the Dragon Reborn—the one person who can fight against the cosmic evil of the Dark One—has traveled to the small village of Two Rivers. Moiraine and the Dark One's army have sensed there are ta'veren in Two Rivers—pattern-changers, around whom the very fabric of fate ebbs and shifts.

Instead of finding one ta'veren in Emond's Field,

however, Moiraine discovers there is a group of young individuals, all born around the same time, all in the same village, who may be the prophesied Dragon Reborn. In *The Eye of the World* (the first book in the series), the individuals in question are friends Rand al'Thor, Perrin Aybara and Mat Cauthon. In the television adaptation, that list is expanded to also include Egwene al'Vere and Nynaeve al'Meara, two women who can channel the One Power and whose fates are also inextricably linked to the fate of the world.

For each of the potential candidates for the Dragon's reincarnated soul, there are these five different drinks, using the same five ingredients (rum, lime juice, soda water, mint and simple syrup) each yielding a different outcome.

DAIQUIRI

INGREDIENTS

- 2 oz rum
- ¾ oz lime juice
- ¾ oz simple syrup
- 1 lime wheel

DIRECTIONS

1. Combine the first 3 ingredients in a shaker with ice.
2. Shake vigorously for 7 seconds and strain up into a coupe.
3. Garnish with a lime wheel.

RUM SMASH

INGREDIENTS

- 2 oz rum
- ¾ oz lime juice
- ¾ oz simple syrup
- 5 pieces of mint (1 for garnish)
- 1 lime wheel

DIRECTIONS

1. Combine the first 4 ingredients in a shaker with ice.
2. Shake vigorously for 7 seconds and strain up into a coupe.
3. Garnish with a mint leaf in the center and a lime wheel.

RUM RICKEY

INGREDIENTS

- 2 oz rum
- ¾ oz lime juice
- 4 oz soda water
- 1 lime wedge

DIRECTIONS

1. Build the cocktail in a highball glass without ice.
2. Add ice, then garnish with a lime wedge.

MOJITO

INGREDIENTS

- 2 oz rum
- ¾ oz lime juice
- ¾ oz simple syrup
- 4–5 pieces of mint
- 1 oz soda water
- 1 lime wedge
- 1 mint sprig

DIRECTIONS

1. Combine the first 4 ingredients in a shaker with ice.
2. Shake vigorously for 7 seconds and strain into a highball glass with fresh ice.
3. Top with soda water, then garnish with a lime wedge and a mint sprig.

RUM MINT JULEP

INGREDIENTS

- 6–8 pieces of mint
- ¾ oz simple syrup
- 2 oz rum
- 2–3 mint sprigs

DIRECTIONS

1. Add mint and simple syrup into a lowball glass or julep cup. Muddle lightly to extract the mint flavor.
2. Add the rum, then top with crushed ice.
3. Garnish with mint sprigs.

The Nightwatcher

INSPIRED BY BRANDON SANDERSON'S
THE STORMLIGHT ARCHIVE

Brandon Sanderson is no stranger to epic series of the fantasy persuasion, and *The Stormlight Archive* is arguably his magnum opus (or will be, once completed). The planned 10-book series follows different characters on Roshar, a planet consumed by powerful, destructive forces and storms. With destruction comes creation, however, and while the storms that dance across Roshar may cause great damage, they also create powerful gemstones imbued with Stormlight that can be controlled by magic workers called Surgebinders.

There are other magics and powers on the surface of Roshar, like the spren, who are splintered-off bits of the powers of creation. It is due to the bond between humans and spren that humans can use stormlight and surgebinding. The Nightwatcher is one such spren who can choose to bless those who seek her out. When she chooses to be found, she provides her seeker a boon but in the same breath also provides a seemingly random (but equally severe) curse. Take, for example, a farmer who sought out the Nightwatcher for a boon to receive a bounty of expensive cloth to sell in order to provide for his family and survive a harsh winter. The Nightwatcher granted this farmer's boon but cursed him to see the world upside down for the rest of his life.

This beverage is designed to mimic the boon Dalinar sought of the Nightwatcher: to end the pain he faces after accidentally causing his wife's death.

> **AUTHOR'S NOTE**
> ....
> Drinking to forget or numb pain is rarely a sound course of action. Try to keep that in mind before paying a visit to the Nightwatcher.

INGREDIENTS

- 1 (750-ml) bottle moonshine
- 1 vanilla bean
- ½ cup brown sugar
- 5 oz soda water
- 1 cherry

DIRECTIONS

1. Pour the moonshine into a container. Slice open and scrape the inside of 1 whole vanilla bean and add it to the container along with brown sugar. Allow the mixture to sit for 24 hours.
2. Strain the mixture back into the original bottle.
3. Pour 2 oz infused moonshine and the soda water into a highball glass and then add ice. Garnish with a cherry.

White Walker Zombie

INSPIRED BY GEORGE R.R. MARTIN'S
A SONG OF ICE AND FIRE

Seemingly the stuff of ancient legend and bedtime stories for bad Westerosi children, the White Walker threat is pretty much ignored by everyone in the Seven Kingdoms (save for some folks in the North—especially those beyond the Wall). The White Walkers are real, of course, and the true threat against which all of Westeros (and Essos, and the rest of the known world) must unite to defeat. Thousands of years before Robert Baratheon took the Iron Throne, the Long Night (aka a very, very long winter) consumed the entire world for a generation, as White Walkers marched across continents, adding to their army of undead in an unrelenting plague of death and despair. In the Battle for the Dawn, somehow the living managed to fight back against the undead hordes, banishing them to the deepest reaches of the Far North, before erecting a wall to keep them away should they ever rise again.

Of course, a wall is a great deterrent, but only as effective as the humans who decide to maintain it. And while the Night's Watch—a force of men responsible for maintaining watch and keeping out White Walkers and wildlings from marching on Westeros—still exists, it's not exactly a formidable army of honorable soldiers. Members swear an oath upon enlistment; the oath allows the recruit to shed their old identity and absolve themselves of any prior crime, while also preventing them from getting married or having children. As one might imagine, the Night's Watch doesn't exactly attract the cream of the crop, so when the men of the Watch claim White Walkers are real and threaten all that humankind holds dear, no one believes them.

But real the White Walker threat is—and under the icy blue gaze of the Night King (the ancient leader of the White Walkers), the horde pushes ever closer to the Wall and the unsuspecting realm beyond.

> **AUTHOR'S NOTE**
> ....
> As Eddard Stark says, winter is coming. And if a generation-long reign of terror is sweeping in, pour yourself a stiff, seasonally appropriate riff on a tiki favorite.

INGREDIENTS

- 1¾ oz vodka
- ½ oz blue Curaçao
- ¾ oz lemon juice
- ½ oz mint or peppermint syrup (or simple syrup and 5–6 fresh mint leaves)
- 1 egg white
- Sour Patch Kids

DIRECTIONS

1. Combine the first 5 ingredients in a shaker without ice.
2. Dry shake for 5 to 7 seconds, then add ice and shake again.
3. Strain up into a coupe and allow the drink to settle so foam forms on top. Serve with a side of Sour Patch Kids (aka White Walkers).

The Red Wolf

INSPIRED BY MARLON JAMES'S **BLACK LEOPARD, RED WOLF**

In Marlon James's *Black Leopard, Red Wolf*, Tracker (aka the titular Red Wolf) narrates a bleak story from his jail cell. Through his recounting, readers learn that he is imprisoned for the murder of a child and hear about his keen sense of smell (which he can use to track and detect across emotion, space and time).

Tracker, as it turns out, has been on a bitter journey of self-discovery. He has not been alone. With Leopard (of the titular Black Leopard), a shapeshifter with whom Tracker shares a complicated and impassioned relationship, Tracker has

been hired to locate a kidnapped child that some very important people want to find. Along the way, there are many other characters Tracker and Leopard encounter as well as plenty of acts of violence and evil and depravity that cross their paths.

Tracker is unreliable as a narrator, unlovable in many ways and even though readers may yearn to find some kind of redemptive quality, some kind of deserving solace in his narrative, James is ruthlessly withholding. Tracker walks the dark spaces that most heroes and villains avoid, and this drink has the same sharp teeth.

AUTHOR'S NOTE
Rooibos, a red tea derived from a South African bush, gives this drink an earthy edge.

INGREDIENTS

- 1 oz rooibos-infused gin
- 1 oz Campari
- 1 oz sweet or rosé vermouth
- 1 orange slice

DIRECTIONS

1. Combine the first 3 ingredients in a lowball glass.
2. Add ice and stir to incorporate.
3. Garnish with an orange slice.

The Lilac Wood

INSPIRED BY PETER S. BEAGLE'S **THE LAST UNICORN**

Perhaps the most beautiful opening line of any fantasy novel belongs to Peter S. Beagle's *The Last Unicorn*. We meet a Unicorn, the last of her kind, who is utterly and totally alone. However, the Unicorn does not really know or care that she is so alone, and until she is warned by a hunter that she may be the last of her kind, she never thinks much of her fellow unicorns. This news distresses her, and she chooses to leave her beautiful lilac wood to learn more. As she continues her search, she discovers that a Red Bull has been gathering the others of her kind and herding them far away, into the sea, for his own pleasure and gain.

Determined to find her fellow unicorns and to stop the Red Bull, the Unicorn and her new friends find his lair, where they face new challenges. Accidentally transformed into a human, the Unicorn learns what it is to love, to experience loss and feel that sting linger. Long after her adventure is over and she returns to her lilac wood, the Unicorn laments she is no longer like others of her kind because of her experience and the knowledge she carries within her heart.

This drink is named for the last unicorn's home—a beautiful, peaceful lilac wood. The drink, like its namesake, is romantic, shimmering and singular. Feel free to share it with others, or enjoy it in contemplative solitude.

AUTHOR'S NOTE

The 1982 animated film of the same name is one of the saddest things this author had ever seen in her young life. Then she read the book and discovered the source material really doubles down on the melancholy.

INGREDIENTS

- 1 oz gin or vodka
- ¾ oz crème de violette
- ½ oz lemon juice
- 1 pinch edible cocktail luster/glitter
- 3 oz sparkling wine

DIRECTIONS

1. Combine gin or vodka, crème de violette, lemon and luster in a stirring vessel with ice and stir lightly.
2. Once chilled, pour into a coupe, then top with sparkling wine, which will keep the glitter moving.

FROM THE BAR

This drink is inspired by the French 75, a World War I-era cocktail made from champagne, gin, lemon juice and sugar.

Six of Crows

INSPIRED BY LEIGH BARDUGO'S **SIX OF CROWS** DUOLOGY

In Leigh Bardugo's second foray into the Grishaverse, she introduces audiences to a ragtag team of six outcasts and one hell of a heist. Set in the international hub of Ketterdam, young mastermind Kaz "Dirtyhands" Brekker accepts a dangerous mission: to raid the impenetrable Ice Court and kidnap a scientist named Bo Yul-Bayur. In return, Kaz and his team will be rich beyond their wildest imagining—if they can live long enough to spend their earnings.

In order to attempt this impossible heist, Kaz forms his dream team: his six crows.

This recipe involves six different drinks all using some of the same six ingredients, each with its unique character twist. As with their namesakes, each of these drinks should be enjoyed together (never try to break up a team like Kaz Brekker's crows).

THE SHARPSHOOTER

Named for Jesper Fahey, a (secret) Grisha who possesses an uncanny ability to shoot with his two revolvers as well as a gambling problem. Jesper provides the gang's comic relief, though he has unexpected depth. He'll also do nearly anything for a pretty face. Like Inej, Jesper's loyalty to Kaz is nearly absolute.

INGREDIENTS
- 1½ oz scotch
- 1 oz sweet vermouth
- ¾ oz lemon juice
- 1 lemon wheel

DIRECTIONS
1. Combine the first 3 ingredients in a shaker with ice.
2. Shake for 7 seconds and strain into a lowball glass filled with ice.
3. Garnish with a lemon wheel.

DIRTYHANDS

Named for the ringleader of the heist, the mastermind behind all of the team's machinations. Kaz "Dirtyhands" Brekker is known for his limp and cane, as well as his ever-present gloves. (Kaz is highly haphephobic— intensely afraid of being touched.) The leader of the gang and the thief who runs the Crow Club, Kaz will do anything, including jobs that are deemed impossible, for the right price. Or for revenge.

INGREDIENTS
- 2 oz scotch
- ¾ oz honey syrup (pg. 134)
- ¾ oz lemon juice
- 1 lemon wheel

DIRECTIONS
1. Combine the first 3 ingredients in a shaker with ice.
2. Shake for 7 seconds, then strain into a lowball glass filled with ice.
3. Garnish with a lemon wheel.

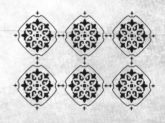

THE HEARTRENDER

A Grisha with heartrender skills (that is, the ability to use magic to manipulate blood, hearts and bodies), Nina Zenik is also a soldier and spy. With her particular abilities—and her tangled relationship with Matthias— Nina makes a dangerous addition to Kaz Brekker's crows.

INGREDIENTS

- 2 oz scotch
- 1 oz sweet vermouth
- 4 dashes aromatic bitters
- 1 brandied cherry

DIRECTIONS

1. Combine the first 3 ingredients in a stirring vessel with ice and stir for 15 seconds or until mixture is very cold.
2. Strain up into a coupe and garnish with a brandied cherry.

THE DEMOLITIONIST

Wylan Van Eck's role to round out the Crows is that of explosives expert. Son of one of the most prominent merchants in Ketterdam, Wylan has connections and a ton of trauma (read: father issues). He is excellent with equations and exceptional at blowing things up.

INGREDIENTS

- 2 oz scotch
- 1 tsp honey syrup (pg. 134)
- 4 dashes aromatic bitters
- 1 lemon or orange peel

DIRECTIONS

1. Combine the first 3 ingredients in a lowball glass with a few pieces of ice.
2. Stir for 10 seconds to dilute, then fill with more ice.
3. Garnish with a lemon or orange peel, expressing the oils over the top for aromatics.

THE WRAITH

Inej "the Wraith" Ghafa is a religious and extremely deadly spy gifted with superb gymnastic skills that are useful for scaling impossible walls, rooftops and the like. Fond of throwing knives, Inej owes her life to Kaz and will follow him to hell and back again.

INGREDIENTS

- 2 oz scotch
- ½ oz lemon juice
- 4 oz ginger beer
- 1 lemon twist

DIRECTIONS

1. Add scotch and lemon juice to a highball glass. Add the ginger beer and stir once to combine.
2. Add ice and garnish with a lemon twist.

THE DRÜSKELLE

Matthias Helvar is a Fjerdan and former witch-hunter. Though it certainly takes him a while to accept his new loyalties, the former holy soldier grapples with his religious beliefs and hatred for Grisha, as well as his feelings for Nina (who, of course, is a witch).

INGREDIENTS

- 2 oz sweet vermouth
- 4 dashes aromatic bitters
- ¾ oz lemon juice
- 4 oz ginger beer
- 1 piece candied ginger

DIRECTIONS

1. In a highball glass, pour in the sweet vermouth, bitters and lemon juice. Add the ginger beer and stir once to combine.
2. Add ice and garnish with a piece of candied ginger.

FROM THE BAR

It isn't called sweet vermouth for nothing—as much as 15 percent of this fortified botanical wine can be made up of sugar. Due to the inclusion of spices— e.g., cardamom, cinnamon or cloves—it's worth trying a few varieties to see what best suits your tastes before splurging on a bottle.

The Chandrian

INSPIRED BY PATRICK ROTHFUSS'S **THE KINGKILLER CHRONICLE**

Every good fairy tale has a force of great and terrible evil. In Patrick Rothfuss's realm of Temerant, that evil goes by many of the aforementioned names, though its most famous—and most feared—is the Chandrian.

A group of seven beings who seem to exist only in myth and fragments of folklore, the Chandrian are considered to be demons and the villains of children's nursery rhymes. But to Kvothe, the prodigious musical talent and brilliant student who claws his way into University, the Chandrian are very real. Kvothe's entire family and Edema Ruh troupe members were murdered by the Chandrian, leaving Kvothe an orphan and filling him with both fear and a desire for vengeance.

INGREDIENTS

- 1 lime
- 1 oz light rum
- 1 oz aged rum
- ¾ oz lime juice
- 1 pinch blue spirulina
- ¾ oz orange spice tea syrup (pg. 134)
- ½ oz green Chartreuse

DIRECTIONS

1. Prepare your garnish by cutting a lime in half, scooping out the citrus pulp from one half and leaving the white rind. Ensure it is dry and set aside.
2. In a shaker, combine the rums, lime juice, blue spirulina and tea syrup in a cocktail shaker with ice.
3. Shake for 5 to 7 seconds, then strain into a highball glass filled with ice. Ensure the ice is stacked to the rim of the glass and then balance the lime shell on the top of the drink (it should float).
4. Fill the lime half with green Chartreuse and carefully light the green Chartreuse on fire. After 1 minute, blow it out and pour the green Chartreuse on top of the cocktail before serving.

FLAME ON

It should go without saying, but when making a flaming lime shell garnish, you'll need to ensure nothing else lights up in the process. The best way to flame the wheel is to light it with a long match, which will give you more room to admire the pyrotechnics from a safe distance. Strike the match, light the green Chartreuse, then sit back and enjoy the show.

FROM THE BAR

Each of the Chandrian is associated with a tell-tale signature, the most infamous of which is a blue flame. While the Chandrian can imbibe this beverage while it's on fire, mere mortals cannot. Extinguish the flame before sipping.

Voldemalört

INSPIRED BY J.K. ROWLING'S
HARRY POTTER AND THE SORCERER'S STONE

Tom Marvolo Riddle. The Dark Lord. He Who Must Not Be Named. Lord Voldemort. The man of many pseudonyms, and the evilest dark wizard of all time, there are few names that conjure more fear than You-Know-Who. Enamored with the Dark Arts and obsessed with discovering the secret to eternal life, Voldemort proudly proclaims he has gone further down the path to discovering unforetold magic to thwart death. Having split his soul into seven Horcruxes (see The Last Horcrux, pg. 34), survived a rebounded death curse and subsisted on unicorn blood in his ethereal form, Voldemort nearly succeeds in his plan to take over the wizarding world (and the Muggle world, for that matter).

This particular drink blends two different notorious inspirations: Voldemort's foulness and Chicago's love-to-hate-it two-fist drinker's liquor. Malört is a Swedish bäsk liquor made with wormwood (and in fact, malört translates to "wormwood"). Astringent, bitter and with an aftertaste that could kill Lord Voldemort were it not for his many Horcruxes, this drink is not for the faint of heart.

> **AUTHOR'S NOTE**
>
> This cocktail is not exactly tasty, nor is it expected to appeal to all palates, but like its namesake and main ingredient, it certainly leaves a lasting impression and may come to haunt you.

INGREDIENTS

- 2 oz Malört
- ¾ oz simple syrup
- ¾ oz lemon juice
- 1 lemon wedge

DIRECTIONS

1. Combine the first 3 ingredients in a shaker with ice.
2. Shake vigorously for 7 seconds and strain into a lowball glass with fresh ice.
3. Garnish with a lemon wedge.

> **FROM THE BAR**
>
> Traditionally, Jeppson's Malört is an integral half of the Chicago Handshake. It is recommended that the drinker chase down the malört shot with a tallboy of Old Style.

TAVERNS

Make it a night to remember
(or forget) by serving up these classic
crowd-pleasing libations.

Pernese Klah

INSPIRED BY ANNE McCAFFREY'S **THE DRAGONRIDERS OF PERN**

In Anne McCaffrey's *Pern* series, readers follow the human colonizers of the planet Pern and their relationship with the planet with a special focus on the humans who bond telepathically with Weyrs (dragons). As the third planet orbiting a Rukbat, a golden star, Pern sounds like (and arguably is) a science fiction series—but the books share much more with fantasy, given that its humans have lost their technology and their history and now live in a pre-industrial world.

And, as with any great fantasy world, there are many foods and beverages native to the planet that have sparked the curiosity of readers. Bubbly pies and meatrolls are ubiquitous over the course of the 24 books that comprise the series, but for every mixed berry tart or grab-and-go meatroll, what truly define Pern is a drink called Klah. A spiced, pungent drink that's best served hot (and often spiked with liquor), Klah is created from the bark of a native Pernese tree. According to the literature, everyone drinks Klah—even children, who take to lightening the brew with sugar and milk.

> **AUTHOR'S NOTE**
>
> Though Klah can be enjoyed at any time of day, a dragonrider most often imbibes this beverage in the morning, right before the binary sunrise from Rukbat and the Red Star rise in the sky. In other words, perfect for brunch.

INGREDIENTS
- 1 oz hazelnut liqueur (e.g., Frangelico)
- ½ oz pimento dram
- 1 oz chocolate milk (dairy or non-dairy)
- 3–4 oz hot coffee
- Freshly grated cinnamon

DIRECTIONS
1. In a mug, add the liqueur and chocolate milk, then pour in the hot coffee and stir.
2. Garnish with freshly grated cinnamon.

al'Thor Hot Apple Brandy Cider

INSPIRED BY ROBERT JORDAN'S **THE EYE OF THE WORLD**

Robert Jordan's *The Wheel of Time* series holds a special place in the hearts of many—across its 14 novels, the saga chronicles the adventures of a group of friends in their struggle to fight against the Dark One. One of these young protagonists is Rand al'Thor, an idealistic, charismatic young man who has simple goals and desires at the outset of his adventure. In *The Eye of the World*, the first book in the series, Rand and his father, Tam, are on their way into the town of Two Rivers from their farm at the outskirts of the isolated community.

The reason for their journey is to make a special delivery of delicious, crisp apple cider to the local inn and tavern proprietress, Mistress al'Vere—just in time for Winternight celebrations.

Before Rand learns he might be the Dragon Reborn, a being destined to fight the Dark One, and before he learns his entire world and parentage are a sham, he's just a young man helping his father while hoping to catch the eye of a girl he admires. A little liquid courage, in the form of this hot apple brandy cider, fits the bill.

> ### AUTHOR'S NOTE
> Take a note from Rand: Some heroes require a little assistance to get their game on. Considering how cider's been enjoyed for more than roughly 2,000 years, it's a tried and true crowd pleaser, a hardy classic that's sure to hit the spot.

INGREDIENTS

- 4 oz apple cider
- ½ oz maple syrup
- ½ oz lemon juice
- 1 cinnamon stick
- 1 piece of star anise
- 3 pieces of allspice
- 2 oz Calvados or other apple brandy
- Apple slice

DIRECTIONS

1. In a small pot or warming vessel, combine the cider with the maple syrup, lemon and spices. Simmer on low for 15 to 20 minutes.
2. Pour the mixture into a mug with Calvados.
3. Garnish with an apple slice.

FROM THE BAR
Don't be afraid to experiment with different forms of brandy when tinkering with this tipple. Applejack is an American-born apple brandy with roots in New Jersey. Alternatively, Calvados, its French cousin, has origins in Normandy.

The Victory of Rurisk

INSPIRED BY ROBIN HOBB'S ASSASSIN'S QUEST

In *Assassin's Quest*, the third book of the Farseer *Trilogy*, FitzChivalry Farseer fights his first true war. In the first battle against the Red Ships, Fitz emerges triumphant—but the price of victory is no small thing. Fitz and his fellow soldiers are numb, hollow and traumatized upon their return to Buckkeep.

Upon their return, every tavern in the realm opens its doors to the triumphant soldiers, and Fitz and his ilk take advantage of their hero's welcome. But as Fitz soon learns, sometimes losing oneself in one's cup is not a balm but an astringent, stinging and causing more damage than good. As Fitz tries to drown out the horrors he witnessed with drink, he also gets caught up in the emotions of all the common folk reveling in the satisfaction of their enemies' slaughter, chugging down the gory details before leaving drunk on bloodlust and booze in equal measure.

War is horror. Fitz learns this truth the hardest way—coming to terms with the aftermath of battle and his own trauma. While this drink is one that might be served in excess at a tavern catering to an army of returning soldiers, Fitz would likely encourage temperance after Rurisk.

INGREDIENTS

- 5 oz ale
- 5 oz lemonade (¾ oz lemon juice, 1 oz simple syrup, 3¼ oz water)
- Lemon wedge

DIRECTIONS

1. In half a Boston shaker with ice, combine ale and lemonade. If using a cobbler shaker, grab another glass to pour into.
2. Using a Hawthorne strainer to hold back the ice in the main shaker, strain the liquid from 1 half of the shaker to the other.
3. Roll the liquid between the 2 halves about 4 or 5 times to chill it, keeping the strainer in place each time to hold back the ice. Strain into a highball glass filled with ice.
4. Garnish with a lemon wedge.

The Prancing Pony

INSPIRED BY J.R.R. TOLKIEN'S **THE FELLOWSHIP OF THE RING**

The most famous fantasy world taverns are often unassuming and only gain renown because of their optimal positioning. Case in point: the Prancing Pony in the village of Bree. Forming an important crossroads between the East Road and the Greenway, Bree (and by extension its local establishment, the Prancing Pony) became a famous way station for Men and Hobbits alike. Because of its location, both planned and (especially) unplanned meetings here can forever change the fate of those in Middle-earth.

Gandalf the Grey, for example, instructs Frodo Baggins (a younger cousin of Bilbo) and his Hobbit companions—Merry, Pippin and

Samwise—to meet him there. While the four Hobbits are pure of heart and work together to protect Frodo from the Black Riders in pursuit, they are decidedly terrible at being incognito. When the Hobbits start to get pushed around by rowdy inn patrons, the Prancing Pony delivers salvation in the form of Strider—aka Aragorn—who recognizes Frodo is carrying the One Ring.

In the Peter Jackson adaptation, Frodo disappears into thin air with the ring on his finger after a failed attempt to get an ale-addled Pippin to shut up. In the book, the proprietors of the Prancing Pony are more helpful, the sort of folks who might offer a beverage like this to weary travelers who need it.

AUTHOR'S NOTE

Hobbits have many strengths and admirable qualities. An ability to seamlessly blend in at a local watering hole without arousing suspicion is not among them.

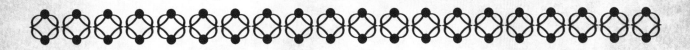

INGREDIENTS

16 oz of your favorite beer or cider
1 oz of your favorite spirit

Recommended Pairings
- *Ale and rye whiskey*
- *Stout and aged rum*
- *Hard apple cider and applejack*

DIRECTIONS

1. Pour your choice of alcoholic beverage into a beer glass.
2. Pour 1 ounce of your favorite spirit into a shot glass. Serve the shot alongside the beer, much as a spirited sidekick accompanies the hero.

FROM THE BAR

A popular pub order, the boilermaker is a "pony"—a 1-oz pour of spirit—served alongside a beer.

Butterbeer

INSPIRED BY J.K. ROWLING'S
HARRY POTTER AND THE PRISONER OF AZKABAN

The first time readers are introduced to one of the magical community's most highly sought-after beverages is at the Three Broomsticks, when third-years Harry, Hermione and Ron have traded Hogwarts for a sojourn into Hogsmeade. Harry, of course, isn't supposed to be at Hogsmeade, given that he doesn't have a signed permission slip from the Dursleys. But thanks to some help from Fred and George Weasley—and Messrs. Moony, Wormtail, Padfoot and Prongs—Harry sneaks out of the castle to join in the fun.

AUTHOR'S NOTE
Readers attempting this concoction are encouraged to source their beer from LGBTQIA-owned breweries and distilleries.

Butterbeer is served at Madam Rosmerta's tavern in hot, steaming tankards—sweet, utterly delectable and warming every bit of Harry from the inside out. Of course, in other asides throughout the series, we learn butterbeer can also be served in bottles (after Gryffindor wins Quidditch matches, the Weasley twins sneak out and ferry some of the precious liquid back), at room temperature or even chilled.

This take on butterbeer can be served hot or cold depending on preference.

INGREDIENTS
- 6 oz pale ale beer
- 1½ oz butter syrup (pg. 134), divided
- 2 egg whites

DIRECTIONS
1. In a pot or warming vessel, add the beer and ¾ ounce syrup and warm for 5 to 7 minutes until there is a light simmer.
2. Meanwhile, in a shaker or mason jar, whip shake egg whites and ¾ ounce syrup until frothed. Pour into a glass and spoon a layer of the foam on top before serving.

The Eolian

INSPIRED BY PATRICK ROTHFUSS'S **THE NAME OF THE WIND**

"**I**sn't this the Eolian? I had heard that this is where pride pays silver and plays golden."

Kvothe is a legend. His exploits, life and triumphs are whispered about in hushed tones throughout Temerant, from the famed University hallways to the inns and taverns of its lesser-known backwaters. Over the course of three nights, an innkeeper named Kote (actually Kvothe in disguise) tells his story plainly to the Chronicler. It begins with Kvothe's childhood as a member of an elite traveling and performing troupe, the eventual murder of his entire family, leading to a hard life on the city streets of Tarbean before finally, finally making his way to University. Kvothe's young life is not easy—for much of his childhood, following the loss of his family, he is starving, always jostling for scraps and forever scavenging to survive.

When Kvothe gets his acceptance to University, things begin to turn around. He's still hard-pressed for coin and constantly worried about how he will study, eat and survive, but University also gives Kvothe an excuse to experience music, his long-lost love. The Eolian, a popular venue and tavern, becomes Kvothe's salvation. Musicians from all corners of the Temerant flock to the Eolian to try to earn their silver talent pipes, a talisman of superior skill that enables its wearer to perform at any tavern for free (and earn wages) and signals the possibility of attracting a noble Patron. The Eolian prides itself on music above all else and welcomes young, nigh-penniless performers, music lovers and exceptionally wealthy patrons alike. It is at this beloved tavern that Kvothe finds his voice, earns his pipes and reunites with a beautiful woman he never thought he'd find again.

AUTHOR'S NOTE

One of the most famous drinks served at the Eolian is Sounten, a trick that serving girls, and Kvothe, use to keep their heads and make a profit. When fans offer to buy Kvothe a round, he orders this expensive drink (which is actually water), splitting the money from the drink with the bar, leaving the fan happy and Kvothe and the house a tad richer.

INGREDIENTS

- 3 oz mead
- ½ oz lime juice
- 3 oz ginger beer
- Candied ginger

DIRECTIONS

1. Pour the first 3 ingredients into a lowball glass.
2. Add ice and top with additional ginger beer if desired.
3. Garnish with candied ginger.

Gigglewater

INSPIRED BY J.K. ROWLING'S
FANTASTIC BEASTS AND WHERE TO FIND THEM

In *Fantastic Beasts and Where to Find Them*, Newt Scamander crosses the pond from London to Manhattan, with his suitcase full of magnificent magical creatures in tow. America, however, is markedly different than Britain—in particular, MACUSA (the Magical Congress of the United States of America) is particularly strict on the segregation of non-magical humans and wizardkind, and unrelenting in its laws and punishment of those who violate said laws. Newt's journey to America takes place in the 1920s, when the great social upheaval that was Prohibition is in full effect for both No-Majs (aka Muggles) and wizards alike.

In order to get their fix of alcohol, folks got creative—pharmaceutical prescriptions of alcohol skyrocketed, as did the proliferation of password-protected hidden bars and lounges (the infamous speakeasy). Newt finds himself in one such NYC speakeasy, the Blind Pig, with his new acquaintance, Jacob Kowalski.

While Newt looks to get some intel from goblin owner and gangster Gnarlak, Jacob sidles up to the bar and tries a glass of gigglewater. Containing pure chortle extract, the bubbly beverage causes its drinker to burst out in, well, giggles.

> **AUTHOR'S NOTE**
>
> Despite being otherwise unyielding with regard to rules, even Seraphina Picquery (President of MACUSA) herself declared that Prohibition laws would not apply when considering gigglewater.

INGREDIENTS

- 3 drops ginseng tincture or extract
- ½ oz green tea syrup (pg. 134)
- 5 oz sparkling wine

DIRECTIONS

1. Combine ginseng droplets and green tea syrup in a champagne flute or coupe.
2. Slowly pour the sparkling wine on top until it reaches the rim.

> **FROM THE BAR**
>
> In the 1920s, "giggle water" was American slang for champagne or liquor.

Ravkan Kvas

INSPIRED BY LEIGH BARDUGO'S **SHADOW AND BONE**

Leigh Bardugo's sprawling Grishaverse—encompassing three separate series, short story collections and a television adaptation—begins with *Shadow and Bone*. In this first book, Alina, an orphan with magical abilities, enlists as a cartographer and, in trying to save her unrequited love and best friend from death at the front lines of a war, exposes herself as a Sun Summoner, one of the rarest and most powerful Grisha in living memory. Swept away into a world of intrigue to hone her magical skills to fight and protect the Ravkan empire, Alina's journey is anything but ordinary.

And yet—despite the grandeur of her new life as a Grisha and the betrayals and challenges that lie ahead of her—at the heart of the story, Alina is a girl who fights to save those under her protection. In order to keep her best friend Mal safe, she enlists in the Ravkan army long before she realizes she possesses any magic. As bedraggled orphans and foot soldiers, neither Alina nor Mal is used to any type of luxury, so it should come as no surprise that the pair has simple tastes in beverages. In Ravka, kvas is the drink of choice. Mildly fermented and homebrewed by farmers and soldiers alike, it has a powerful kick.

> ### AUTHOR'S NOTE
> Kvas is meant to be shared—make sure to pass the bottle around.

INGREDIENTS

- 16 cups water
- 4 slices rye or pumpernickel bread
- ½ cup berries (blackberries work best)
- ¾ cup honey
- 1 Tbsp active dry yeast

> ### FROM THE BAR
> This riff on the traditional eastern European kvass should be refrigerated and will keep for up to a week.

DIRECTIONS

1. Boil water in a large pot. Remove from heat. Meanwhile, toast bread slices (burnt slices are optimal for flavor) and tear each slice into quarters.
2. Place the bread and berries in the hot water. Cover tightly with a lid or wrap to seal, then allow to sit in a warm place at room temperature for 2 days. On the third day, taste the mixture. If desired, let it sit for another day for more flavor.
3. Strain the mixture through a cheesecloth. Be sure to finely strain it a few times to remove all the crumbs.
4. Mix the honey and yeast, then stir into the strained liquid. Cover again and allow to sit for 1 day, stirring at least once over a 24-hour period.
5. Taste the kvas. If you desire more carbonation, let it sit for another day. Once you are satisfied, transfer it into 2 large plastic bottles and seal them (leave some space at the top for the carbonation). Refrigerate for 1 day and enjoy.

Gimli's Gauntlet Gimlet

INSPIRED BY J.R.R. TOLKIEN'S *THE LORD OF THE RINGS* TRILOGY

Gimli, son of Glóin of the House of Durin, has a proud lineage. Tracing his ancestors back to Durin I (Durin the Deathless), Durin III (the Dwarf who wielded the most powerful of the seven Rings of Power given to the Dwarves) and Thorin I (of The Hobbit), Gimli has dwarven royal blood, though he himself is not royalty. Ultimately more important to Middle-earth than his kin, Gimli stands on his own as a member of the Fellowship of the Ring and is a pivotal fighter in the War of the Ring.

> **AUTHOR'S NOTE**
> Drinking games with friends are always encouraged—though, drinker, beware! This ale syrup take on a gimlet is stronger than your typical tankard of beer.

In the Peter Jackson film, Gimli is often paired with Legolas in good-natured competition—the number of Uruk-hai slain at Helm's Deep, for example. In the extended cut of *The Two Towers*, Gimli throws down a different gauntlet for his elven BFF: a last-man-standing drinking contest. While Gimli is a connoisseur of ale and certainly knows his way around a tavern, Legolas is able to eke out the victory (although, thanks to Legolas's elvish constitution, it's not much of a competition).

INGREDIENTS

- 2 oz gin
- 1 oz lime juice
- ¾ oz ale syrup (pg. 134)
- Lime wheel

DIRECTIONS

1. Combine the first 3 ingredients in a shaker with ice. Shake vigorously for 10 seconds. Strain straight up into a coupe.
2. Garnish with a lime wheel.

Olau Hot Toddy

INSPIRED BY TAMORA PIERCE'S
THE SONG OF THE LIONESS QUARTET

Every young hero deserves a wise mentor. Alanna, masquerading as "Alan" in an attempt to earn her shield and become a knight of the realm, faces a number of obstacles on her path to autonomy. First, there's the problem that women aren't allowed to become knights. Second, there's the reality that Alanna is smaller and less trained than the other boys in both matters of physical and political skill. While Alanna owes much of her success to her fierce determination, another large part is due to the friends and mentors she makes along the way.

Enter Sir Myles of Olau: scholar, noble, knight and unexpected pacifist. As Baron of Olau, a grand estate in Tortall, Myles does not lack for wealth or power. And yet, throughout the series, especially in Alanna's first year of training, Myles urges his students to challenge the norm, to think differently, to question the status quo with a lens of equity and justice. Myles takes a shine to young Alanna, showing her his ancestral home and its apple orchards—and though he does not out her, Myles also is one of the first to know Alanna's true nature.

Upon her first visit to Barony Olau—what will one day become her inheritance—Alanna wins a magical sword, Lightning, at great peril. Myles gently coaxes a shell-shocked Alanna back to her senses by serving her a toddy.

> ### AUTHOR'S NOTE
> The hot toddy is believed to have its origins in India (derived from the Hindi taddy, a drink made with fermented sap), though a rival school of thought claims that Irish doctor Robert Bentley Todd prescribed the beverage to his patients.

INGREDIENTS

- 4 oz water
- ¾ oz honey syrup
- ½ oz lemon juice
- 1 cinnamon stick
  Tea bag (to flavor the water), optional
- 2 oz whiskey, brandy or mead
  Lemon slice pierced with 4–5 cloves

DIRECTIONS

1. In a small pot or warming vessel, combine water, honey syrup, lemon juice, cinnamon stick and tea bag (if using). Simmer on low for 15 to 20 minutes.
2. Pour the mixture into a mug with your spirit of choice.
3. Garnish with a clove-pierced lemon slice.

FROM THE BAR
Make this non-alcoholic by using more water in place of alcohol. For more flavor (and caffeine), steep the water with black tea.

DRINKING SLANG THROUGH THE AGES

Because ye olde drunkards had plenty of ways to get pixilated (buzzed).

Antifogmatic *(c. 18th century)* Liquor consumed for the sole purpose of keeping one warm in fog or other damp weather. Precisely the sort of thing you'd want to down before strolling within a swamp, cave or misty meadow.

Blootered *(c. 16th century)* "Blooter" was once used to describe a loud fool and later took on a verb usage. In its current form, this Scottish term now applies to anyone who is especially inebriated. In Ireland, it reappeared as "peloothered" *(1914)*.

Bousy *(1529)* The original form of "boozy" has Dutch roots: "booze" *(c. 1325)*, once a verb, derives from the Middle Dutch "būsen": to drink too much. In his early 18th-century poem "The New Dunciad," Alexander Pope includes it as "bowsy."

Cock-eyed *(1926)* Ernest Hemingway used this in *The Sun Also Rises* as a means of drawing attention to an inebriated person's peepers. Similar iterations include "owl-eyed" and "pie-eyed" *(1904)*.

Note: Ever the literary legend, Hemingway referred to his hangovers as "gastric remorse."

Dead Man *(c. 17th century)* A fittingly morbid name for a most dreadful sight: an empty bottle of beer or liquor. Also appears as "dead marine" *(1831)* or "dead soldier" *(1917)*.

Fou *(1535)* A Scottish derivation of "full," it appears in the Robert Burns poem "Death and Doctor Hornbrook" *(1785)* to describe the inebriated narrator, who encounters Death after a heavy night of drinking. Still currently used in the delightful expressions "blin fou" (much like it sounds: "blind drunk") and "fou as a puggie" (the less obvious "drunk as a monkey"). It would not be out of place for the likes of Professor McGonagall or perhaps even Hagrid to incorporate it. It also means "crazy" in French (having derived from the Latin "follis"), but let's not bring Fleur into it.

Humpty-Dumpty *(c. 17th century)* According to the *Oxford English Dictionary*, the tragic character of English nursery rhymes shares a name with a 17th-century drink composed of ale boiled with brandy. (On that note: please drink responsibly, lest you fall off a wall and crack your skull.)

Juiced *(1946)* Chester Himes, author of the *Harlem Detective* series, used "juiced up" when referring to intoxicated people. But juice in reference to alcohol goes back much further: Patriot polymath Benjamin Franklin referred to drunk people as "juicy" as far back as 1737 in "The Drinker's Dictionary," published in *The Pennsylvania Gazette* (which you should read online posthaste and which absolutely contains the gem "[He's] Half Way to Concord," among others).

Katzenjammer *(c. 1834)* From the German for "a cat's misery," it's since been used by English speakers to describe a cacophony of noise as well as the raging hangover one receives after indulging in the strong stuff.

Nobbler *(1842)* It might sound like a beast Newt Scamander would have stowed away in his suitcase, but this noun of Australian origin refers to a serving of an alcoholic beverage.

Nippitaty *(c. 16th century)* Though its origins remain murky according to Merriam-Webster, this noun is used in reference to delicious, strong liquor, most notably for ale.

Pissed *(1812)* While American readers would believe this adjective has something to do with being angry, this synonym for drunk is of British origin, meaning it wouldn't be out of place in either Red London, White London, Black London or Grey London. It also appears in the colorful phrase "pissed as a newt" *(1957)* (or, if you're in Australia, "pissed as a parrot").

Pixilated *(1848)* Though it bears an entirely different connotation—and visual—for 21st-century readers (given how out of sorts you might feel after a few drinks), this term originally blended "pixie" and the suffix "-ated," the latter of which is possibly a nod to the word "elated." Used to describe that high-spirited (if bewildered) buzzed feeling. Here's hoping the fey approve.

Popskull *(1867)* Poorly (and often illegally) distilled whiskey. Likely a nod to how your head will feel after a few swigs.

Rotgut *(1633)* Terrible, low-grade liquor that's almost guaranteed to do to sully your intestines. But it will get you drunk. Also appears the other way around as "gut-rot" *(1916)*.

Stewed *(1737)* A cooking-related take on the word drunk. Later iterations include "corned," "pickled" and "salted."

Sting *(1927)* No, it's not just the name of the Elven sword Frodo wields—it's also an Australian noun used for methylated spirits, or the type of hooch that can also thin paint.

Tarantula Juice *(1861)* Poor-tasting cheap whiskey, possibly named for such a drink's "bite." Similar terms include "snake juice" *(1890)* and "panther juice" *(1929)*.

The Jim-Jams *(1885)* Originally a reference to delirium tremens, or the shaking and hallucinations that occur after drinking a great deal, typically as a form of withdrawal.

Tipsy *(1577)* Of course you know what this word means—what's astounding is that it's been in use since the 16th century. By the 19th century, a "tipsy cake" referred to a sweet baked good soaked in alcohol.

Boozy Fantasy Terms That Should've Been

For reasons that remain unknown, the following terminology and euphemisms don't appear in the works below but feel like many a missed opportunity.

Harry Potter
- knocked off their broom
- Polyjuiced
- Transfigured
- fang of the basilisk

The Lord of the Rings
- precious potion
- one drink to rule them all
- gone halfway to Mordor
- is fluent in Quenya

The Witcher
- bewitched
- coin-tossed
- mutated
- chasing the Wild Hunt

The Chronicles of Narnia
- had one too many Turkish delights

COURTS

When you're looking to impress a refined,
discerning crowd, these top-notch tipples
are guaranteed to make a scene.

The Law of Surprise

INSPIRED BY ANDRZEJ SAPKOWSKI'S **THE WITCHER**

The Law of Surprise is a custom within the world of *The Witcher*, often invoked to great dramatic effect. Usually, the custom takes form when someone comes to another's aid, and the party being aided has nothing to give to their savior in return. The Law of Surprise, therefore, is a kind of carte blanche mixed with Russian roulette. The nuance for the Law of Surprise is that language truly matters: A Witcher may invoke the custom by requesting the first thing that greets you, or by asking for something that the rescued party does not expect. This could take the form of a beloved dog, or, more frequently, the unborn first child of the rescued party.

In Geralt's case, the infamous law comes into play when he is traveling to Cintra and is invited to a banquet in which suitors apply to marry the Queen's heir, Pavetta. Unfortunately, this results in her marriage to the cursed Duny, the Urcheon of Erlenwal. For his part in helping Duny and Pavetta celebrate their love, Geralt reluctantly invokes the Law of Surprise—tying his destiny forever to their then-unborn daughter, Ciri, who will one day come to be known as the Lion Cub of Cintra.

> **AUTHOR'S NOTE**
>
> At its heart, the Law of Surprise is a loaded boon that looks like one thing but often is revealed to be something completely different. In this cocktail's case, the drink looks like a martini but is in actuality a negroni.

INGREDIENTS

- **1 oz rosemary-infused gin**
- **1 oz bitter bianco**
- **1 oz bianco vermouth**
- **1 lemon twist**

DIRECTIONS

1. Combine first 3 ingredients in a stirring vessel with ice. Stir for 15 seconds and strain into a coupe or martini glass.
2. Garnish with expressed lemon oils over the top, twist the lemon peel and drop into the glass.

> **FROM THE BAR**
>
> You can swap out the bitter bianco for Suze, another bitter liqueur made from gentian—just be sure to use ¼ oz Suze for every oz.

Phial of Galadriel

INSPIRED BY J.R.R. TOLKIEN'S *THE LORD OF THE RINGS* TRILOGY

A light to use in dark places, the Phial of Galadriel was a boon presented to Frodo Baggins on his arduous quest as ringbearer to destroy the One Ring. Containing the light of Eärendil's star—preserved light from the Two Trees of Valinor—Galadriel's gift eases Frodo's burden as he and the Fellowship of the Ring depart the refuge of Lothlórien.

Encased in glass, the light would prove useful to both Samwise and Frodo on their journey, long after the splintering of the Fellowship. Upon entering Mordor through Gollum's intentional trap, Frodo and Sam use the Phial to thwart the giant spider Shelob, using its light as a weapon to drive her back. When Frodo's burden becomes too heavy, especially in the presence of the Nazgul, the light of Eärendil helps Frodo resist the ring's call. The Phial is one of the few items Sam and Frodo keep following the completion of their deed in *The Return of the King*: Along with Frodo and Bilbo, the Phial travels Westward to end their time on Middle-earth and fade. Leaving Middle-earth isn't necessarily just a sad thing; on the contrary, only few can travel to the Undying Lands, having earned an eternal respite in paradise.

AUTHOR'S NOTE

For a cocktail to glow in the darkest night, simply use tonic water, which glows under a blacklight bulb. The shimmer dust is the second bit of icing on this particular cake.

INGREDIENTS

- 2 oz gin
- 6 oz tonic
- ¼ oz lemon juice
- Pinch edible shimmer dust

DIRECTIONS

1. Build the cocktail in highball glass, add ice and stir.
2. Turn off the lights and use a blacklight to illuminate the shimmering drink.

FROM THE BAR

Most edible shimmer dust is a combination of cornstarch, sugar and color additives. Just make sure the label says "edible" and not "non-toxic," which is not FDA-approved.

The Huntress (Feyre)

INSPIRED BY SARAH J. MAAS'S
A COURT OF THORNS AND ROSES

Sarah J. Maas's brand of romantic fantasy is at its best with her *A Court of Thorns and Roses* series, following a young human woman's struggles to keep her family safe and adjust to her new reality as an immortal member of the Fae. But before she becomes a Queen of the Spring Court and the Night Court, she is first and foremost simply Feyre, the huntress. Gifted with a strong heart and the ability to track and hunt even the fiercest of predators, Feyre earns the ire of the fey folk when she kills a wolf who is not just a wolf. In recompense for her actions, she is taken from her ailing father and sisters and whisked away to the faerie world of Prythian where danger lurks around every possible corner.

But Feyre is no stranger to darkness and the burden of responsibility; her family once was rich and prosperous, thanks to her father's dealings as a merchant. All of that changed in Feyre's early life when her vain mother died of typhus (though not before making Feyre, the youngest of her children, promise to take care of the family) and her father made a bad deal that left the family bankrupt. Since the age of nine, Feyre has learned she must provide for a family that cannot provide for themselves—and so she grows strong and does what needs to be done.

AUTHOR'S NOTE

This drink, a tribute to the First High Lady of Prythian, has roots in Feyre's origins as a huntress—never weak, never tamed and never broken.

INGREDIENTS

- 2 oz aged rum
- ¾ oz lemon juice
- ¾ oz chai syrup
- 1 oz white wine float
- 1 egg white, optional

DIRECTIONS

1. Combine rum, lemon and chai syrup with ice in a shaker (if using egg white, dry shake before adding ice).
2. Shake vigorously for 7 seconds and strain into a lowball glass over ice.
3. Slowly pour the white wine float on top (it will layer).

FROM THE BAR

Whether you're vegan or just not a fan of raw egg in your drinks, a good substitute for egg white is aquafaba, the liquid from canned chickpeas that can be whipped up like meringue.

Rose Sharbat

INSPIRED BY TASHA SURI'S **THE BOOKS OF AMBHA**

Tasha Suri's *Books of Ambha* follow a young woman, Mehr, who walks a tricky balance between Ambha and Amrithi. The illegitimate first daughter of a noble caste father and desert-dweller mother, Mehr has struggled with the expectations placed on her by Ambhan society. As a descendant of gods, the Daiva, on her mother's side, Mehr's blood and true calling is a powerful thing. It is so powerful, in fact, that when Mehr performs a ritual during a dreamstorm, the Maha (the ruler of all Ambha) notices and comes to collect. Seemingly immortal, the Maha bested

Mehr's ancestors long ago and is determined to maintain that power at all costs.

Forcing Mehr to leave her home and come to his court as the wife of Amun, one of his most powerful henchmen, the Maha has grand plans to harness her Daiva-born power. Though Mehr has grown up in relative finery while still understanding that she is different and all the nuances of her station, the Maha's palace is a shock—the Maha's table is finer than anything she has ever experienced, and though hungry and thirsty, she knows that the lavish display is also an assertion of power over Mehr and Amun.

> ### AUTHOR'S NOTE
> Amidst the fragrant meats, stews and grains, this rose sharbat is a courtly temptation ripe for the picking.

INGREDIENTS

- 2 oz rose hip-infused vodka or rose hip tea
- 1 oz lemon juice
- 1 tsp fig jam
- 3 oz tonic water
- Dried rosebuds

DIRECTIONS

1. If using vodka, infuse 1 Tbsp dried rose hip (or 1 rose hip tea bag) with 8 oz vodka. Let steep for 20 minutes and remove.

2. In a shaker, combine lemon juice, jam and vodka or tea with ice. Shake and strain into a highball glass with ice.

3. Top with tonic water and garnish with dried rosebuds.

FROM THE BAR
Fruity, tangy and loaded with vitamin C, rose hips are used to make a myriad of delicious goods, including bread, jam, soup, syrup, beer and wine.

Jadis (The White Witch)

INSPIRED BY C.S. LEWIS'S **THE CHRONICLES OF NARNIA**

The White Witch is best known for her actions in *The Lion, the Witch and the Wardrobe* (see Edmund's Temptation, pg. 76), but she plays a larger, earlier role in the shaping of C.S. Lewis's work. In *The Magician's Nephew*, the sixth book in the series (but first in terms of overall timeline), Jadis's formidable backstory is revealed. A royal and heir to the world of Charn, Jadis learned to wield powerful and dark magic before her reign of relentless winter in Narnia. Determined to rule and best her sister at all costs, Jadis masters a great and terrible spell that would kill every living entity in the world except for the speaker. This spell—the Deplorable Word—was Jadis's great trump card against defeat.

> **AUTHOR'S NOTE**
>
> A queen who would rather kill her world than admit defeat—who would turn her subjects to stone for displeasing her—this cold, cutting drink is for you, Jadis.

But as she and her sister fought for power to rule Charn, Jadis's forces were crushed (though arguably, her sister violated the pact to refrain from using magic in battle first). Rather than let her sister win—rather than surrender—Jadis does the unforgivable and becomes Queen of Charn. A desolate, lifeless world, Jadis places herself under a spell to preserve herself until some future time when future travelers might enter Charn and trip her alarm—by ringing a bell, the spell on Jadis would be broken, and she would emerge from her lifeless slumber to rule over the world that dares intrude on her own. (And of course, that bell is in fact rung in *The Magician's Nephew* by a young Digory Kirke.)

INGREDIENTS

- 1 oz vodka
- 1 oz kirsch
- ½ oz maraschino liqueur
- ¾ oz lemon juice
- 1 egg white
- Lemon peel

DIRECTIONS

1. Combine first 5 ingredients in a shaker without ice and dry shake vigorously for 5 seconds.
2. Add ice to the shaker and shake again for 7 seconds.
3. Strain up into a coupe and express lemon oils over the top. Discard the lemon peel before serving.

The Dance of Dragons

INSPIRED BY GEORGE R.R. MARTIN'S *FIRE & BLOOD*

George R.R. Martin's *Fire & Blood*—and the television adaptation, *House of the Dragon*—details the spectacular civil war that tears the Targaryen dynasty and its dragons apart. Following King Viserys I's death, a bitter succession struggle ensues in which Viserys's named heir, his first child and daughter Rhaenyra, tries to hold on to her legacy against her half-brother Aegon II, born of Viserys's second wife and Rhaenyra's childhood friend, Alicent Hightower.

This vicious war would leave many of the Targaryen line dead. This includes most of Rhaenyra and Alicent's children and nearly all their dragons, all casualties of violence, poison and treachery. The war would not only affect the Hightowers and Targaryens; the whole of the Seven Kingdoms bear the crushing price of the conflict, suffering the fallout from dragonfire, destroyed cities and killed crops for decades to come.

Perhaps most importantly, the war also sets a precedent for women who might dare to try to hold the Iron Throne: Fearing calamity similar to Rhaenyra's troubled reign, nearly all future Targaryen females—even if they may be eldest and rightful heirs to the throne—are placed behind their male relatives in succession to power.

AUTHOR'S NOTE

This flashy beverage captures the essence of all the fire and death of the Dance of Dragons—sans the male primogeniture.

INGREDIENTS

- 1 oz mezcal
- 1 oz reposado tequila
- ¾ oz lime juice
- ½ oz grapefruit juice
- ¾ oz cherry syrup
- A lime half turned inside out to make a shell
- ½ oz overproof tequila

DIRECTIONS

1. Combine first 5 ingredients in a shaker with ice. Shake vigorously for 7 seconds. Strain into a lowball glass with ice.
2. Place the lime shell on top of the drink and fill with the overproof tequila. Carefully light on fire and allow to burn.

FROM THE BAR

Do not drink while the cocktail is on fire. Either allow the flame to extinguish or blow it out before pouring the tequila into the drink and consuming.

Ring of Barahir

INSPIRED BY J.R.R. TOLKIEN'S *THE SILMARILLION*

Finrod was Galadriel's brother (see Phial of Galadriel, pg. 68), and while his role in Middle Earth is completely glossed over and minimized in the television show *The Rings of Power*, he is a pivotal piece in the shape of things to come. A great king of Nargothrond, making friends with Dwarves and Men despite the Elves' natural predilection toward condescension, Finrod was fair and open in his dealings with Middle-earth's other races.

In the great war against Morgoth (the greatest evil and darkest of lords), Finrod would have perished had it not been for rescue at the hands of Barahir of House of Bëor. In return for this life-saving aid, Finrod swore an oath to Barahir, presenting him with his own ring featuring two serpents representing the bond between Elves and Men. This symbolic gesture would travel down the generations through the hands of the Bëor, ultimately landing with Aragorn, who in turn gifts the ring to the beautiful Elf Arwen. Much like its namesake ring, this cocktail is best prepared and given to someone whom you wish to serve.

> **AUTHOR'S NOTE**
>
> Like his sister Galadriel, Finrod bestows lavish gifts on the deserving.

INGREDIENTS

- 1 tsp edible golden shimmer dust
- 1 tsp sugar
- 1 tsp salt
- 1½ oz gin
- ½ oz Midori
- ¾ oz lime juice
- ½ oz safflower syrup
- 2 skewered cherries

DIRECTIONS

1. Mix the shimmer dust, sugar and salt and rim a coupe or martini with the mixture.
2. Combine the gin, Midori, lime juice and safflower syrup in a shaker and shake vigorously for 10 seconds.
3. Strain up into the prepared coupe and garnish with a skewer with 2 cherries.

FROM THE BAR

A Japanese melon liqueur, Midori (from the Japanese for green) was introduced to the U.S. market in 1978 at Studio 54 as part of a party for the cast and crew of the film *Saturday Night Fever* (1977).

The Spring King (Tamlin)

INSPIRED BY SARAH J. MAAS'S *A COURT OF THORNS AND ROSES*

Tamlin, the High Lord of the Spring Court, is cursed. The youngest of three brothers, Tamlin was never intended to become the High Fey and Lord of his father's court. But when his mother, father and brothers are killed by the King of the Night Court (in recompense for the murder of his own wife and daughter at the hands of the Spring Court), Tamlin becomes the only heir. With his court in disarray—no one wants to pledge fealty to the bestial youngest son who never learned the ways of court— Tamlin makes a further mess of things by antagonizing Amarantha, Queen of

AUTHOR'S NOTE
....
This drink pays homage to Tamlin's court by mixing spring flavors with a beastly kick.

Under the Mountain, by spurning her advances. Placing a powerful spell on Tamlin and the remnants of his court, Amarantha curses the Spring King by telling him he has seven years to find a human woman with hatred in her heart for the Fae and earn her love in return for his own—otherwise he and all of his people will be her prisoners forever.

In classic fairy tale fashion, Tamlin does find a human woman with hatred in her heart (see The Huntress, pg. 69). But loving her, and earning her love, is no small feat. Good thing the determined Spring King is up to the challenge.

INGREDIENTS

3–4 **snap peas**
2 **oz gin**
¾ **oz simple syrup**
¾ **oz lemon juice**
1 **snap pea on a skewer**

DIRECTIONS

1. Place the snap peas in a shaker and lightly muddle.
2. Add the gin, simple syrup and lemon juice to the shaker with ice. Shake vigorously for 10 seconds. Strain up into a coupe or martini and garnish with a snap pea on a skewer on the rim.

Edmund's Temptation

INSPIRED BY C.S. LEWIS'S **THE CHRONICLES OF NARNIA**

*T*he Lion, the Witch and the Wardrobe is a formative series for any intrepid fantasy reader. C.S. Lewis's series follows the four Pevensie siblings and their adventures into Narnia. After being shipped off to live with Professor Digory Kirke in the English countryside to escape the German bombings of London, the four children discover a wardrobe in the house actually leads to a strange, magical world. Lucy Pevensie, the youngest of the siblings, travels to Narnia first, meeting a satyr named Mr. Tumnus, and brings her sister and brothers to follow soon after.

As magical and wondrous as Narnia may be, the creatures and inhabitants of the realm actually live in fear of their ruler, Jadis, the White Witch and Queen of Narnia.

Under Jadis's rule, Narnia has been forced into winter for a hundred years—and while most of the Pevensies recognize that Jadis is the true cause of the misfortune that has befallen Narnia, one of the siblings stands apart.

Edmund Pevensie, third in age of the four children, is ripe for the White Witch's picking. While Peter, Susan and Lucy are steadfast against Jadis, the Witch approaches Edmund with a proposal. Using a box of Turkish Delights (a delicate rosewater-sweetened candy that reminds Edmund of earlier, untroubled time with his parents and siblings from before the Blitz), Jadis promises Edmund he will become a Prince, at which point he can have as much Turkish Delight as he wants.

> **AUTHOR'S NOTE**
>
> Is it truly Edmund's fault that he succumbs to a desire that was magically and strategically designed to exploit his weaknesses? This courtly drink is an ample temptation for any young would-be magical traveler.

INGREDIENTS

- 1 oz lemon juice
- 3 drops rose water
- ½ oz simple syrup
- 5 oz tonic
- Dried rosebuds or rose petals (**organic only**)

DIRECTIONS

1. In a highball glass, build the drink with lemon juice, rose water and simple syrup.
2. Add the tonic, then add ice. Garnish with rose petals on the sides of the glass or float dried rosebuds on top.

> **FROM THE BAR**
>
> Rose water lends a delicate floral note to light, refreshing cocktails. It pairs well with gin, dry vermouth, rosé, champagne, prosecco, tequila and vodka.

The Fall of Gilead

INSPIRED BY STEPHEN KING'S **THE DARK TOWER**

In *The Dark Tower*, Roland Deschain is the last of the Gunslingers, a legendary force of peacekeepers from a kingdom called Gilead, in All-World. Stephen King's version of the knights of the round table, Gunslingers were diplomats, mediators and leaders who would train from childhood and were forced to pass trials in order to earn their guns. Should a would-be gunslinger decide to abandon their training, they would become a mere aristocrat. Should an aspiring gunslinger fail his trial, he would be exiled from Gilead and sent west to roam All-World, Mid-World and the Wastelands in between.

In *Wizard and Glass*, the fourth book of the *Dark Tower* series, readers learn more about the enigmatic antihero at the heart of the series through Roland's tale of his youth, his lost friends and his lost love. Just as his ka-tet (a group bonded by fate) of Eddie, Susannah, Jake and Oy listen to Roland's story, so too do we readers learn of the rise and fall of Roland's Gilead and the growing power of the forces of darkness with the Crimson King and his all-seeing eye.

The Dark Tower is a mashup of Western and post-apocalyptic fantasy, and this courtly drink pays homage to both genres with an elegant take on a cowherd's special: ranch water.

> ### AUTHOR'S NOTE
> Take the Gunslingers' teachings in mind as you prepare this drink: Aim with your eye, shoot with your mind and kill with your heart.

INGREDIENTS

- 2 oz tequila
- ¾ oz lime juice
- 5 oz flavored soda water (your favorite)
- 1 lime wedge

DIRECTIONS

1. Build first 3 ingredients of the cocktail in a highball glass with ice.
2. Garnish with a lime wedge.

Might vs. Right

INSPIRED BY T.H. WHITE'S *THE ONCE AND FUTURE KING*

There are many reasons why T.H. White's *The Once and Future King* novels are exceptional and foundational fantasy books. One of the main reasons is the thematic struggle Arthur has with "might" (rule by force) and "right" (rule with justice). From his youth, Arthur (or the Wart as he's known almost exclusively in *The Sword and the Stone*) has the benefit of training and learning from Merlyn, who forces Arthur to question his assumptions and the rule of others. As a boy, Arthur sees that his elder brother, father and knights of stories frame the world through a "Might is Right" perspective—ruling through force, fear and brute strength. Through Merlyn's lessons (transforming the Wart into a fish, a bird or other fantastical exercises), Arthur learns the value of Right and ruling with Justice.

Learning about concepts is very different than putting them into practice, however, as Arthur soon learns. He grapples with these two different, wildly opposed forces throughout his rule, sometimes coming up with great innovations as a politician at the Round Table, though he lacks sorely in execution, a flaw that becomes his downfall (see that whole Lancelot/Guinevere thing).

> ### AUTHOR'S NOTE
> This drink embraces these two opposing forces: might (strength, in the form of a high-proof liquor) and right (the cocktail equivalent of justice).

INGREDIENTS

- 1 oz rye
- 1 oz Grand Marnier
- 1 oz lemon juice
- 1 lemon wheel

DIRECTIONS

1. Combine first 3 ingredients in a shaker with ice. Shake vigorously for 7 seconds and strain up into a coupe or martini glass.
2. Garnish with a lemon wheel on the rim of the glass.

FROM THE BAR
If you like your drinks on the sweeter side, substitute the Grand Marnier (a cognac-based triple sec blend) for Cointreau (which is just triple sec). Just bear in mind you'll lose out on the darker, robust tones of the former.

The Night Court (Rhysand)

INSPIRED BY SARAH J. MAAS'S **A COURT OF THORNS AND ROSES**

Rhysand is the heir of the Night Court and incredibly powerful as both a fighter and a leader. Tamlin (see The Spring King, pg. 75) and Rhys were friends, once upon a time, before the mutual destruction of both of their families at the hands of the other. Enemies at the outset of *A Court of Thorns and Roses*, the two Kings vie for the future of their people—and eventually, for the favor of Feyre (see The Huntress, pg. 69).

When Feyre first meets Rhysand in *A Court of Thorns and Roses*, she does not trust his motives in wanting to help her best Amarantha, though eventually she accepts his aid in order to confront the Queen Under the Mountain and save her beloved Tamlin. As payment for his help, however, Feyre owes Rhys a week of her life each month and bears the mark of his help as a permanent tattoo on her body. The two share a telepathic bond that will prove powerful beyond the bond that the Spring King has with the new Fey High Queen.

> **AUTHOR'S NOTE**
>
> Dark, handsome, sensual and completely devoted to Feyre—the Night King is the whole package and it is little wonder that he wins the girl's heart at the end.

INGREDIENTS

- 1½ oz black strap rum
- ¾ Oloroso sherry
- ¼ oz honey syrup
- 3 dashes mole bitters
- 1 orange peel

DIRECTIONS

1. Combine first 4 ingredients in a stirring vessel with ice. Stir for 10 seconds and strain into a lowball glass with ice.
2. Express the orange peel over the top and discard the peel.

FROM THE BAR

The word sherry is the anglicized pronunciation of the Spanish *(vino de) Xeres* or "(wine from) Xeres," the former spelling of the city of Jerez, Spain, where sherry is sourced.

POTIONS

Bountiful botanicals and spices set the
tone for these enchanting elixirs, designed
to ensnare the senses with every sip.

Potion of Giant Size

INSPIRED BY WIZARDS OF THE COAST'S
DUNGEONS & DRAGONS

In Wizards of the Coast's Dungeons & Dragons fantasy roleplaying game, the potion of giant size is a magical concoction that, when consumed, grants the character the ability to become a giant (with all the accompanying physical changes and benefits, and occasionally setbacks). It's an especially handy thing to have on hand when a party needs immense strength or size or a quick exit from a low-ceilinged dungeon.

Similar to other potions or spells in D&D, however, there are some notable risks and potential drawbacks depending on the player (see Red's Fireball, pg. 106). Drastically increased size and strength can be difficult to control, and as a result, the newly transformed giant character may unintentionally cause damage to their surroundings or allies. It is important, therefore, to make sure the right player gets the potion—if your Game Master is kind enough to plant one for your party to find.

The potion itself is described as being pale and milky and brewed—of all sources—from a giant clam's tongue. It is notable for its powerful effects as well as its equally powerful aroma, which reeks of rotting algae. The cocktail version of this potion (albeit sans clam) is not for the faint of heart—cumin gives the drink a giant punch.

INGREDIENTS

- 5 oz milk of choice
- 2 oz whiskey
- 1 oz simple syrup
- ¼ tsp cumin

DIRECTIONS

1. Combine ingredients in a shaker with ice and shake vigorously for 7 seconds.
2. Strain into a lowball glass, mug or flask—your call.

The Dresden Aphrodisiac

INSPIRED BY JIM BUTCHER'S **STORM FRONT**

Chicago private eye and wizard Harry Dresden is often hired to crack supernatural mysteries and crimes. Sometimes business is slow, but sometimes it explodes chaotically with several opposing parties pursuing conflicting interests around the same case. In *Storm Front*, the first book in the *Dresden Files* series by Jim Butcher, it's certainly the latter. Harry is hired by Monica Sells to find her missing husband, Victor, who appears to have been a normal human but recently discovered his magical abilities after losing his job and has since been trying to expand said abilities. Harry is also called upon by Lt. Karrin Murphy of the Chicago P.D. when two people are found dead, mid-coitus, with their hearts ripped out. To make matters all the more complicated, Harry is also approached by John Marcone, mob and drug lord of Chicago, who wants Harry to stop helping the police.

As he dives into the case, Harry decides to proactively make an escape potion (should he need to make a quick getaway) but needs the help of an air spirit named Bob in order to remember the steps and ingredients that will work. Bob, who rags on Harry for his lack of a love life, tells Harry that he'll only help him if he also makes a love potion simultaneously. Tired, frustrated and finding it easier to go along with Bob rather than argue, Dresden agrees.

In any alchemical potion-making, certain ingredients are required: sensory ingredients (one for each sense) and a component for both the mind and soul. In Harry/Bob's version of a love potion, the ingredients comprise conventional sensory ingredients like perfume, dark chocolate and shredded lace. There are unconventional items as well: a shredded $50 bill (in lieu of diamond dust) and the ashes of a racy romance novel (in lieu of a passionate love letter). Most importantly, Dresden's version of the potion uses a base of tequila (though any other liquor as well as Champagne could also be used to help lower inhibitions).

> **AUTHOR'S NOTE**
>
> This version of Dresden's alchemical aphrodisiac is a play on the classic, trashy-in-all-the-right-ways chocolate martini.

INGREDIENTS

- 1½ oz vodka
- ½ oz white crème de cacao
- ½ oz Chambord
- 1 oz cream or milk
  Grated white chocolate or white chocolate shavings

DIRECTIONS

1. Combine first 4 ingredients in a shaker with ice and shake vigorously for 7 seconds. Strain into a coupe or martini glass.

2. Garnish with a dusting of grated white chocolate or white chocolate shavings.

Blinkmoth Serum

INSPIRED BY WIZARDS OF THE COAST'S **MAGIC: THE GATHERING**

In the multifaceted worlds of Magic: The Gathering, there are many creatures and planes of existence. With Scars of Mirrodin: The Quest for Karn, players are introduced to a world in which organic creatures are recombined with metals to wield magic. Throughout Mirrodin, there are glowing fireflies called Blinkmoths that are both beautiful and powerful. Representing the very essence of magic within Mirrodin, these gentle swarms dance across the surface of the metallic plane, performing alluring, moving acts of dance.

AUTHOR'S NOTE

Blinkmoth serum glows blue-white, which this cocktail mimics—without the extreme addictiveness or environmentally destructive aftereffects of its namesake.

When a Blinkmoth is separated from its swarm, it dies, producing a small amount of a serum called Lymph. Through experimentation and chance, Vedalken scientists learn the serum grants its drinker huge advantages including sharper mental acuity and self-realization. To take advantage of these properties, the Vedalken took to larger scale experiments and harvesting of Blinkmoths, ultimately destroying the population of Blinkmoths, much to the detriment of Mirrodin.

INGREDIENTS

Honey

Toasted coconut

2 oz butterfly blue pea flower-infused gin

½ oz coconut water syrup

3 dashes orange bitters

DIRECTIONS

1. Prepare a martini glass or coupe by dipping or painting the rim with honey and then rolling it in (or sprinkling it with) toasted coconut.
2. Combine remaining ingredients in a stirring vessel with ice. Stir for 10 to 15 seconds until chilled and strain up into the glass.

FROM THE BAR

Native to Indonesia, the butterfly pea plant produces vivid blue flowers that are commonly used in drinks throughout Asia as well as in rice dishes (yes, blue rice!). When a small amount of lemon juice is added to butterfly pea tea, the deep blue drink turns purple in seconds. A botanical ingredient, it pairs well with gin and vodka.

Chalice Honey Mead

INSPIRED BY ROBIN MCKINLEY'S *CHALICE*

Robin McKinley is an old standby in fantasy literature, known for her books for younger readers as well as her knack for detailing delicious food and drink. McKinley's work also extends to adults, including the standalone novel *Chalice*, which may be her most mouthwatering book to date.

The plot centers on a woman named Mirasol, newly appointed to the role of Chalice. Her responsibility is to bind her folk and their land to their Master. As a mere beekeeper by training, this is no small feat. However, there's a new Master of the Willowlands—the former Master, his brother, having died suddenly and unexpectedly—who also happens to be a Priest of Fire. This is unprecedented and unwelcome (his touch is fiery death), especially for Mirasol's hive, and she is placed in the delicate situation of wanting to give him a fair shot while also needing to appease her people.

As in her other books (like cinnamon rolls in *Sunshine*, for example), food/drink is an integral part of the McKinley sensory reading experience. In Mirasol's case, that integral ingredient is honey, captured in this incredible mead.

AUTHOR'S NOTE

Mead is another word for a honey wine. Sweet and simple at its essence (honey, water, yeast), mead can be made unique by adding different fruits or spices to the fermentation process.

>>>>>>>>>>>>>>>>>>>>>>>>>>>>>>>>>>>>>>>

INGREDIENTS

- 3 oz mead
- ¼ oz pimento dram
- 1½ oz Manzanilla sherry
- 1 orange peel

DIRECTIONS

1. Combine the first 3 ingredients in a stirring vessel with ice. Stir for 10 to 15 seconds until chilled and strain up into a wine glass.
2. Garnish by expressing the oils of the orange peel over the drink. Discard the peel.

FROM THE BAR

Pimento dram is a simple liqueur flavored with pimento berries, aka allspice. It lends a bold, spicy note to drinks and shines when used to cut through sweeter ingredients like mead.

Fire Heart

INSPIRED BY NAOMI NOVIK'S **UPROOTED**

The Dragon in Naomi Novik's *Uprooted* is an irascible man. Or at least, it certainly seems that way to Agnieszka (Nieshka), as he seems annoyed that she can work magic and that he has to take her—rather than an exceptional/beautiful village girl—to his tower. At first, Nieshka is convinced that if she can just stay out of the Dragon's way, he won't require anything of her; she follows the notes left to her from the Dragon's previous girls, making sure to cook him his meals, drop them off in the library, then run away. Unfortunately for Nieshka, that advice only works if you don't possess magic. Soon, Agnieszka is learning cantrips and spells that exhaust her or don't feel right and that she can't ever seem to perform correctly.

In between her time recovering from the Dragon's draining magical lessons, Nieshka also explores her new home, finding a room filled with several different potions. One of them turns anyone who inhales its fumes to stone (see Bottle of Mist, pg. 94), while others possess powerful healing properties. The most rare of all these potions, though, is the Fire Heart potion: liquid molten fire which will burn greedily through even the most evil of tinder. Nieshka sees firsthand what Fire Heart can do when she takes it to stop an assault of the Wood's wolves on her village, using the potion to burn through the corruption that has tainted the animals and town. The Dragon, of course, is irritated when he learns of Nieshka's actions because Fire Heart is exceptionally rare and hard to get right—10 years' worth of cultivation goes into the smallest vial. Inspired by the Dragon's hard-earned recipe, this take on Fire Heart uses Chartreuse, a spirit whose centuries-old instruction for concoction is known only by two monks at a time.

> ### AUTHOR'S NOTE
> While it may be desperately hard to create Fire Heart, and absolutely should be used wisely, never forget that a potion is meant to be used. Share this elixir with friends (even if you choose to guard the recipe).

INGREDIENTS

- 1½ oz reposado tequila
- ½ oz sweet vermouth
- ¾ oz green Chartreuse
- 1 orange peel

TOOLS

- Matches or lighter

DIRECTIONS

1. In a stirring vessel, combine the tequila and sweet vermouth. Stir with ice and hold.
2. Pour the green Chartreuse into the glass and carefully light it on fire. Allow it to burn for at least 10 seconds. Extinguish the flame by pouring the chilled mixture from the stirring vessel over the green Chartreuse.
3. Garnish by flaming the oils of an orange peel and twisting the peel into the drink.

FROM THE BAR

There are six types of tequila: blanco (unaged), reposado (aged up to 1 year), añejo (aged for 1 to 2 years), extra añejo (aged for 3 years or more), cristalino (an aged tequila filtered through charcoal) and joven (a blend of blanco and an aged tequila). Like wine, its flavors become complex over time.

Eldritch Horror

INSPIRED BY KIERSTEN WHITE'S *HIDE*

Known for her young adult historical and speculative fiction, Kiersten White's first adult audience novel explores Lovecraftian horror, dreadful family secrets and an overrun amusement park. *Hide* begins with the chance of a lifetime: 14 strangers enter the long abandoned Asterion Amazement Park to play a game of hide and seek on a reality television show to win $50,000. Or, at least, that's what each of the contestants has been told. Most of the competitors are of the social media influencer or influencer-adjacent variety (a CrossFit instructor, an actress, a Banksy-wannabe), though there are some odd other entrants: an app developer, a writer, the nicest gas station attendant you will ever meet in your life, a veteran and a cult survivor. And then there's Mack, the main point of view character of the book, who survived her father's murderous rampage by hiding in their small family house. Mack is now experiencing homelessness and is determined beyond all measure to win the prize money.

Soon, Mack and the others learn that the "reality television show" and "contest" have never been real. Something sinister is seeking the humans trapped in the park, and it is not of this world. As Mack and her allies try to uncover the truth, they come face-to-face with a monster—an eldritch, Lovecraftian horror whose very appearance is enough to drive the beholder mad. This potion is a toast to Asterion's founding families and the horror that has been conjured in the lost amusement park, with a perfect bitter twist.

> **AUTHOR'S NOTE**
>
> When faced with the opportunity to strike a Faustian bargain for riches, glory, the proliferation of one's bloodline, etc., the author reminds you to carefully consider both the short- and long-term costs.

INGREDIENTS
- 2 oz apple-infused whiskey
- ½ oz demerara syrup
- 3 dashes bitters
- 1 cinnamon stick

TOOLS
- Matches or lighter

DIRECTIONS
1. Combine first 3 ingredients in a stirring vessel with ice and stir for 10 seconds. Strain into a lowball glass filled with ice.
2. Light one end of the cinnamon stick. It takes about 15 to 20 seconds for the cinnamon stick to start to burn. Place the lit cinnamon stick on top of the ice (if it sticks out above the cocktail) or balance it on the rim of the glass. Allow the cinnamon stick to fully extinguish before drinking.

Lucy's Cordial

INSPIRED BY C.S. LEWIS'S **THE CHRONICLES OF NARNIA**

In C.S. Lewis's first adventure into Narnia, *The Lion, the Witch and the Wardrobe*, the Pevensie children are transported from London to a countryside manor to escape the Blitz, where they are then transported again to a magical land of eternal winter. In their travels to Narnia, the children learn a little something of treachery, loyalty and justice as they discover the extent of the White Witch's evil ways (see Jadis, pg. 71).

Although winter is the constant season in Narnia, thanks to the White Witch's control, Christmas never takes place, as Father Christmas has been barred from entering the realm for 100 years by the time the Pevensies arrive. One of the first signs of Jadis's crumbling power is when Father Christmas arrives on the scene, bearing gifts for all of the young human children. To Lucy, the youngest of the Pevensie clan, he gifts two important items: a dagger and a bottle of cordial.

The latter is exceptionally powerful and rare, formed from the juice of Fire-Flowers, which grow on the mountains of the sun. Using this elixir, limited though it may be, would allow Lucy to bring the drinker back from certain death and cure nearly any ailment or injury. This version of Lucy's Cordial uses goldenrod tea as an earthbound substitute for those who may not be able to traverse the mountains of the sun to gather Fire-Flowers.

> ### AUTHOR'S NOTE
> In the grand canon of fantasy potions, Lucy's Cordial ranks among the most powerful for its unparalleled healing capabilities.

INGREDIENTS

- 4 oz goldenrod tea
- 3 oz milk
- ½ oz honey (or more to taste)
- 1 oz goldenrod tea-infused vodka, optional
- Foamed milk, optional

DIRECTIONS

1. Boil water and allow tea to steep. Meanwhile, in a separate pot, warm (but don't boil) the milk on low heat.
2. In a mug or teacup, add the tea, milk, honey and vodka if using. Stir to mix. If desired, garnish with a spoonful or 2 of foamed milk.

FROM THE BAR

Rich in antioxidants, goldenrod tea has been used in folk medicine as a diuretic and a means to treat various infections. It has an anise-like flavor.

Milk of the Poppy

INSPIRED BY GEORGE R.R. MARTIN'S
A SONG OF ICE AND FIRE

George R.R. Martin's *A Song of Ice and Fire*, related books as well as the television adaptations of *Game of Thrones* and *House of the Dragon* showcase a violent fantasy world torn apart by political turmoil, fantastical supernatural creatures and war. A common potion that appears in all of Martin's various media adaptations is a dangerous and highly addictive palliative drug: Milk of the Poppy.

A powerful narcotic used to numb pain and induce sleep, the thick, purple liquid is often administered with wine (with or without the subject knowing). Produced by the Maesters—that is, educated scholars who serve as advisors and healers in the Seven Kingdoms—Milk of the Poppy is prescribed to help ailing Westerosis with anxiety, pain and childbirth...and is sometimes used as a lethal poison.

> **AUTHOR'S NOTE**
>
> This milky, numbing, highly dangerous drink is not to be imbibed lightly. This cocktail is free of Martin's narcotic and poisonous side effects, but that does not mean it won't pack a punch.

INGREDIENTS

- 1 oz poppy seed syrup
- 5 oz milk
- ¼ tsp hibiscus powder
- 2 oz unaged fruit brandy, optional
  Poppy seeds

DIRECTIONS

1. Combine syrup, milk, hibiscus and brandy if using in a shaker with ice. Shake vigorously for 7 to 10 seconds and strain up into a lowball glass.
2. Garnish with a pinch of poppy seeds.

The Golden Son

INSPIRED BY LAINI TAYLOR'S **STRANGE THE DREAMER**

Laini Taylor spins magic and dreams with her *Strange the Dreamer* duology. Before Lazlo Strange leaves his home to discover the secrets of the city known only as Weep (see The Floating City of Weep, pg. 103), before he understands his true destiny, before all of that, Lazlo is just a young man with a head full of dreams. A war orphan, Lazlo grew up under the tutelage of monks, listening to stories of magic. At the age of 13, however, Lazlo discovered the Great Library and found a new passion and home for all of the stories he so yearned to learn. And so, Lazlo left the monastery behind, becoming an apprentice librarian.

Lazlo isn't the only character in *Strange the Dreamer* with something to prove, however; there is also Thyon Nero, the second (and golden) son of the Duke of Vaal, who's already a legend at age 15. A student of the noble art of alchemy, Thyon is able to transmute—which is to say, transform—lead into bismuth. For this accomplishment, he is rewarded by the Queen with a laboratory where he works diligently to discover even greater secrets. What nobler pursuit for the boy with hair so golden that the queen wore his shorn locks as a necklace than to discover the secret to transmuting lead into gold?

Like so many others, Lazlo is taken with Nero, and after witnessing Nero's father beating him for his continued failures to turn lead into gold, Lazlo gives Nero the missing piece to accomplish this impossible task (incongruously, discovered in a children's book). Nero kicks Lazlo out, but just weeks later, the golden son is able to accomplish the greatest alchemical feat…thanks to Lazlo, of course.

Inspired by Thyon Nero's impossible task, this drink is vibrant and golden, transforming the mundane into something remarkable.

AUTHOR'S NOTE

This cocktail uses a secret ingredient just as Nero did to transmute the impossible— but in this drink, it's all about turmeric.

INGREDIENTS

- ¼ tsp turmeric
- 8 oz milk of choice
- 2 tsp light brown sugar
- Pinch black pepper
- 2 oz aged rum, optional
- Pinch cinnamon

DIRECTIONS

1. Combine first 4 ingredients (and rum if using) in a pot and place on the stove to warm. Whisk until the mixture is hot.
2. Pour into a mug and garnish with a pinch of cinnamon.

FROM THE BAR

A fixture of Chinese and Ayurvedic medicine, turmeric has long been prized for its anti-inflammatory properties and earthy taste.

Bottle of Mist

INSPIRED BY NAOMI NOVIK'S **UPROOTED**

Naomi Novik's rather prolific pen takes on Eastern European folklore with her *Uprooted* duology, comprising *Uprooted* and its companion novel, *Spinning Silver*. In *Uprooted*, Novik's story centers on a young woman named Agnieszka (Nieshka). Her small village rests precariously at the edge of the deep, dark woods, and she is scared—not for herself, but for her beautiful, brave best friend, Kasia. You see, the woods are magical and malevolent, and in order to protect themselves, Agnieszka's village has made a pact with a Dragon (who isn't really a dragon but a wizard). Every 10 years, the Dragon selects one of the village's young women to serve him in his

tower. After the period of servitude is up, the young women are released back to their homes—but they are forever changed.

Nieshka is terrified her dearest friend will be chosen by the Dragon—how could she not be, with her grace and goodness? Despite these fears, in a shocking twist, the Dragon selects Nieshka instead.

Swept away to the Dragon's lair, Nieshka learns nothing is what it seems. For example, she inexplicably has the ability to command magic. In one of her first forays into potions, she accidentally shatters a bottle of mist, one whiff of which can freeze the individual unfortunate enough to smell it (in this case Nieshka) in time.

> ### AUTHOR'S NOTE
> This "drink" is actually a bottled liquid that can be incorporated into multiple beverages—and best of all, it won't turn you to stone. Use it to prep glassware before you pour in a drink, to add an element of spice aromatics on the top of a cocktail or to spritz on as a fresh garnish.

INGREDIENTS
- 8 oz overproof rum
- 1 Tbsp cloves
- 1 Tbsp whole allspice
- 4 cinnamon sticks
- 3 pieces star anise

TOOLS
- Food grade 2 oz spray bottle

DIRECTIONS
Combine all ingredients in a mason jar and allow to sit for up to a week. For best results, shake or agitate the jar once a day to mix up the flavors and keep the infusion consistent.

FROM THE BAR
Use this to line the glass for the Eldritch Horror (pg. 90) or The Gloom (pg. 96). Or top off a cocktail with a spray as a garnish on the Goblet-Chilled Sangria (pg. 122) or Pernese Klah (pg. 52).

Dried Frog Pills

INSPIRED BY TERRY PRATCHETT'S **DISCWORLD** SERIES

Sir Terry Pratchett's work is renowned across genres, but his most well-loved is arguably the *Discworld* series. Zany, expansive, hilarious and exceptionally clever, *Discworld* tells the tale of a planet that balances atop four elephants atop a turtle. There are 41 *Discworld* novels, and while the majority can be read on their own without needing to follow a prescribed order, several of the books follow certain mini-arcs that tie them together. One such mini-arc is that of the wizards of Unseen University, following the exploits of the zany faculty of wizards who run the school, one of which is the Bursar.

At Unseen University, in order to secure a faculty seat, it is typical for the incumbent to be assassinated. For Professor A.A. Dinwiddie, DM (7th), D.Thau., B.Occ., M.Coll., the Bursar role was perfect—when the previous Bursar was killed in action while trying to save the library, Dinwiddie succeeded him. Though Dinwiddie doesn't have much of a stomach for action or treachery, he knows the Bursarship is a wildly unpopular job that no one else could want, and he happens to be ecstatic at the potential of a future summing numbers and maintaining balances. Of course, all of that changes when a new Archchancellor is appointed for the University, making the Bursar's life a living nightmare. Over time, Dinwiddie feels his mind gradually eroding, his hold on sanity slipping away with every outlandish action of the Archchancellor.

In order to maintain his tenuous grasp on sanity, Dinwiddie takes a healthy dose of dried frog pills: hallucinogenic medicine that sometimes allows the Bursar to hallucinate that he is sane. (A lot of the time, he ends up hallucinating that he can fly, for example, which is no good for him or the faculty.)

This drink version of the Bursar's frog pills uses green spirulina to mimic the amphibious coloring of its inspiration and will certainly render you healthy, minus the hallucinations, when taken daily.

AUTHOR'S NOTE

The phrase "to go Bursar" —a common colloquialism in *Discworld*'s city of Ankh-Morpork, meaning "to go insane"—is inspired by poor Dinwiddie and is part of his Unseen University legacy.

INGREDIENTS

  Pinch green spirulina
½ oz pineapple juice
½ oz apple juice
¼ oz lime juice
½ oz choice of vodka, tequila or gin

DIRECTIONS

1. Combine all ingredients in a shaker with ice.
2. Shake vigorously for 7 seconds and pour into a shot glass.

FROM THE BAR

For an early morning pick-me-up, skip the booze and sub in coconut water.

The Gloom

INSPIRED BY SILVIA MORENO-GARCIA'S
MEXICAN GOTHIC

A horror-fantasy novel written in the gothic tradition but set in the 1950s, Silvia Moreno-Garcia's *Mexican Gothic* follows young, educated socialite Noemí Taboada, whose latest joys in life center upon little acts of rebellion against her family (her father, really) and the expectations they have for her. All of that changes when Noemí and her father receive a letter from Cousin Catalina begging for help, as she suspects her new husband is poisoning her. At her father's request, Noemí leaves her comfortable life of parties and flirting to rush to her cousin's aid, trading cosmopolitan society for the distant mountain town of El Triunfo. When Noemí arrives at Catalina's new home, called High Place, she instantly knows something is wrong—Virgil Doyle, Catalina's husband, is controlling, patronizing and raises all of Noemí's hackles. According to Virgil, his family and their doctor, Catalina is suffering from consumption and should not be disturbed.

As Noemí is, infuriatingly, kept away from her cousin, she begins to dig at the foundations of High Place and the Doyle family. She learns the ancestral home was transported from Europe to the Mexican countryside and contains more than just Virgil's deceit: among the decaying beams and rotted wallpaper, there is also a dusting of gold—the gloom—generated by a special kind of fungus that affords great power and control to the men of the Doyle line. It's a hallucinogenic drug that is wielded by the patriarchs for terrible ends—unless Noemí can break the cycle and save her cousin.

> ### AUTHOR'S NOTE
> This cocktail is glittery gold and has its roots in smoky mezcal, a perfect complement for the shimmering gloom that threatens to consume Noemí and the people she loves.

INGREDIENTS

- 1½ oz mezcal
- ½ oz amaro (like Cynar)
- ½ oz sweet vermouth
- 3 dashes orange bitters
- Pinch gold shimmer dust

DIRECTIONS

1. Combine all ingredients in a stirring vessel with ice. Stir for 10 to 15 seconds until chilled.
2. Strain up into a coupe or martini glass.

FROM THE BAR
From the Nahuatl word "mexcalli," which means oven-cooked agave, mezcal is a smoky spirit made from distilled agave (not unlike tequila).

Formula 86

INSPIRED BY ROALD DAHL'S **THE WITCHES**

In middle-grade fantasy-horror novel *The Witches*, a young boy named Charlie learns witches are real, and a very real threat at that. An orphan who is taken in by his grandmother, Charlie hears firsthand about the evils of witches—demons with an insatiable hate for children—and also how to keep himself safe from them. For the most part, his grandmother's advice is helpful.

When the pair go on a seaside vacation, Charlie learns there are several female convention attendees in town—members of the Royal Society for the Prevention of Cruelty to Children—and susses out that they are actually witches.

> **AUTHOR'S NOTE**
>
> This version of Formula 86 is, true to spirit, kid-friendly and should appeal to younger palates. As an added bonus, consuming it will not transform you into anything other than a happy imbiber.

The icing on the cake is the fact that the Grand High Witch, the most evil, powerful and important witch in all the world, is at the hotel as well. Eavesdropping on their convention in the hotel ballroom, Charlie learns they have a grand master plan that they will be putting quickly into action: purchasing sweet shops across England and giving away free chocolates. Not just any chocolates, of course, but treats poisoned with Formula 86, which happens to turn the person consuming the potion into a mouse. When the child transforms into a mouse, the witches hope that the child's teachers, parents and friends will kill them.

INGREDIENTS

- 1½ oz chocolate syrup
- 3 oz milk
- 2 drops orange blossom water
- 1½ oz aged rum, cognac, añejo tequila or whiskey, optional
- 5 oz soda water

DIRECTIONS

1. Combine first 3 ingredients (and spirit if using) in a beer glass and stir until incorporated.
2. Pour in half the soda water and beat into the mixture to create the foam on top.
3. Pour in the remaining soda water and stir once.

Liquid Luck

INSPIRED BY J.K. ROWLING'S
HARRY POTTER AND THE HALF-BLOOD PRINCE

In the penultimate volume of the *Harry Potter* series, Harry, Hermione and Ron (unbeknownst to them) spend their last full year at Hogwarts and make a great number of different revelations. Fresh off of earning their Ordinary Wizarding Levels (O.W.L.s), the sixth-years now must narrow down their class selections to focus on their future careers. Harry, having earned an Exceeds Expectations in Potions, thinks his future as an Auror (aka Dark Wizard catcher) is at an end, given that Professor Snape, the Potions Master, sneered that he would only accept an Outstanding O.W.L. for his N.E.W.T. (Nastily Exhausting Wizarding Test) students. Happily, Harry learns he actually can continue with Potions under the new Master, Professor Slughorn, and joins the class, though he has none of the textbooks or tools. Slughorn gives Harry a loaner copy of *Advanced Potion-Making*, one that happens to be helpfully covered in notes and masterful adjustments to Libatius Borage's text, authored by the self-proclaimed "Half-Blood Prince."

In his very first day of class, Professor Slughorn (recently coaxed out of retirement by Dumbledore) offers up an enticing opportunity for his students. They are all to create a Draught of Living Death, and the best concoction will win an exceptional prize: a small vial of Felix Felicis, aka Liquid Luck. Harry follows the scribbled instructions from the Prince and manages to win. The possibilities for using the potion are dizzying for young Harry—as Slughorn says, a small dose of Felix will make an ordinary day extraordinary.

Clear, warming and filling its drinker with instant confidence and prowess, Felix Felicis is meant to be enjoyed sparingly. Drink too much of it and the user will be prone to recklessness and dangerous overconfidence. This cocktail is much of the same: A martini can give you the confidence you need and result in an extraordinary adventure, if brewed correctly and used in the appropriate dosage.

AUTHOR'S NOTE

Liquid luck = liquid courage.

INGREDIENTS

- **2** oz gin or vodka
- **1** oz vermouth
- **3** dashes orange bitters
  Olive, cocktail onion or lemon twist

DIRECTIONS

1. Combine first 3 ingredients in a stirring vessel with ice. Stir for 10 to 15 seconds and strain up into a martini glass or coupe.

2. Garnish with an olive, cocktail onion or lemon twist.

FROM THE BAR

Ordering a martini can be a personal experience, in part because the drink has so many well-established variations. Here's how to get what you want.

◇◇◇◇◇◇◇◇◇◇◇◇◇◇◇◇◇◇◇◇◇

CLASSIC

A martini with the ratio of gin or vodka to dry vermouth at 2 oz to 1 oz or 3 oz to 1 oz (a vodka-based martini is called a Kangaroo)

DRY

Very little dry vermouth (less than ½ oz)

EXTRA DRY

Barely any to no dry vermouth

WET

More than 1 oz of dry vermouth

DIRTY

Olive brine in place of dry vermouth

50/50

Half vodka or gin and half dry vermouth

STRAIGHT UP

Stirred and poured into the glass without ice

ON THE ROCKS

Stirred and strained over ice

TWIST

Lemon peel garnish

OLIVES

Olive garnish, typical for a dirty martini

GIBSON

Cocktail onion garnish

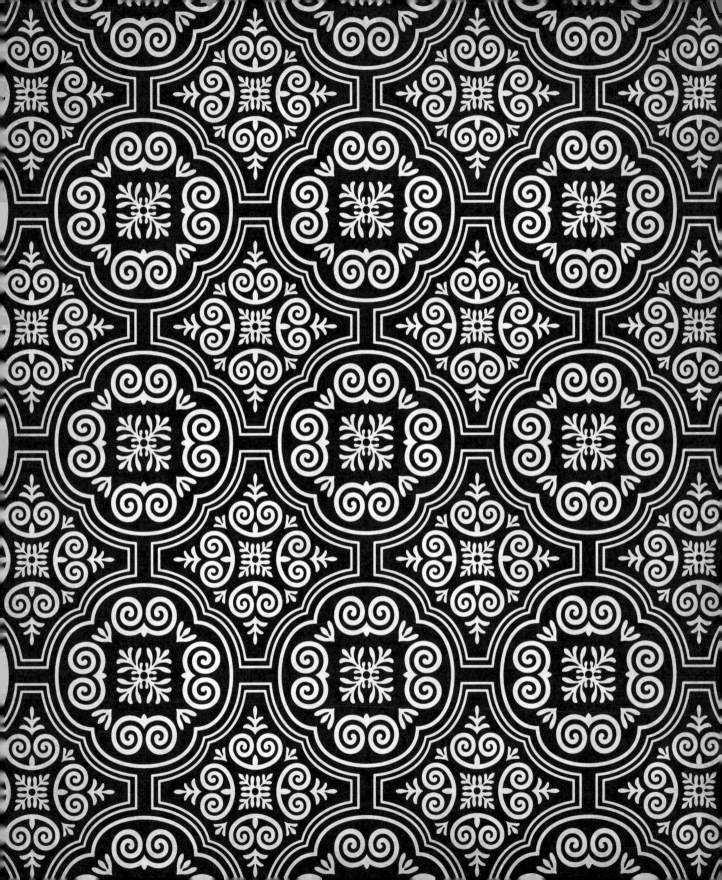

SPELLS &
CURSES

These bewitching brews are sure
to enchant even the most discerning
palates, so choose wisely.

Sign Magic (Aard, Axii, Igni, Quen, Yrden)

INSPIRED BY ANDRZEJ SAPKOWSKI'S **THE WITCHER**

Andrzej Sapkowski's *The Witcher* is a multimedia fantasy success. Before leaving the page to grace television screens, Geralt of Rivia made an indelible mark on fans through video games. In each of the three *Witcher* video games, players control Geralt and chart the course of his decisions across different missions and adventures. Of course, part of the joy of playing Geralt in each game is unleashing some of the Witcher's magical powers, notably in combat with monsters. While Witchers aren't particularly adept magic-workers (unlike, say, sorcerers and sorceresses), they utilize sign magic to enhance their battle prowess.

Over the course of the first game, players unlock each of the five signs Geralt can wield to fantastic effect:

Aard: a wave of psychic energy that can knock back enemies or objects

Axii: a charm that can make a friend of an enemy (for a short time)

Igni: a classic flame damage spell

Quen: a shielding spell

Yrden: a ground sigil that prevents anyone from crossing it

> ### AUTHOR'S NOTE
> Sangrita is a traditional accompaniment to a shot of quality tequila. Each of the five signs gets its own sangrita variation below, so (like Geralt) you can be the master of your own destiny.

INGREDIENTS
SANGRITA

- 1 jalapeño
- 15 oz tomato juice
- 6 oz lime juice
- 6 oz orange juice
- 1 tsp white pepper
- 1 tsp black pepper
- 1 tsp kosher salt
- 1½ oz tequila

DIRECTIONS

1. Slice jalapeño and add slices, stem and seeds to pitcher with remaining sangrita ingredients. Stir and allow to sit for 4 hours.
2. Taste for spice level, and if you want more of a kick, allow to sit for another 2 hours.
3. Strain the sangrita through a fine strainer or cheesecloth. Keep refrigerated until serving. When ready, fill 1 shot glass with sangrita and another with tequila. Sip the sangrita then the tequila, alternating until finished.

CHOOSE YOUR SIGN

- **Aard (spicy):** add 1 tsp cayenne powder
- **Axii (fruity):** substitute pineapple juice for tomato juice
- **Igni (smoky):** add a few drops of liquid smoke (taste test for intensity)
- **Quen (savory):** use only 11 oz tomato juice and add 4 oz spinach or kale juice
- **Yrden (refreshing):** use only 10 oz tomato juice and add 5 oz cucumber or celery juice

The Floating City of Weep

INSPIRED BY LAINI TAYLOR'S **STRANGE THE DREAMER**

Two hundred years have passed since a mysterious city disappeared from the face of the world, and 15 years have passed since the memory of the city's name was plucked from the minds of anyone who tried to recall it. Instead, when anyone attempts to summon the name of the lost city, it is replaced with a single word: weep.

Lazlo Strange has long been fascinated by tales of magic and mystery, especially the aura surrounding the lost city now known simply as Weep. As the saying goes, the dream chooses the dreamer, and Lazlo dreams always of Weep. Since the day the name of the city was stolen from his mind, he has devoted his life to discovering the truth. As a librarian, Lazlo searches for any history of Weep and its lost people, its language and the seraphim and mesarthim rumored to roam its gilded streets. One day, adventure rides into Lazlo's life—literally—when the legendary Godslayer Eril-Fane and his soldiers arrive in Lazlo's city, looking for scholars to join their party bound for Weep. Desperate to catch a glimpse of the city and discover its hidden secrets, Lazlo joins the Godslayer's party and finally finds the truth of Weep, as well as its curse, floating among the clouds.

> ### AUTHOR'S NOTE
> While the secrets of Weep require long years of study, concocting this briny beverage is shockingly straightforward.

INGREDIENTS
- 2½ oz vodka or gin
- ½ oz olive brine or salted water
- Herb-infused olive oil

DIRECTIONS
1. Add the first two ingredients to a stirring vessel. Fill the vessel halfway with ice and stir for 15 seconds. If the sides of the vessel are not yet cold, stir for another 7 seconds.

2. Strain into a coupe and garnish with 5 to 6 drops of herb-infused olive oil.

Blackthorn's Bargain

INSPIRED BY JULIET MARILLIER'S
BLACKTHORN & GRIM

Juliet Marillier is no stranger to spells and curses throughout her extensive, exquisite fantasy novels. In *Dreamer's Pool*, the first book in the *Blackthorn & Grim* series, Marillier takes readers to a magic-imbued medieval Ireland. A healer has been imprisoned by a lord and left to rot in a dungeon for a crime she did not commit (as he tries to hide his own crimes of raping women with impunity). Blackthorn, as the woman chooses to call herself, focuses on her rage and desire for revenge to keep herself going, even when things look their most dire, most notably when she learns the lord plans on having her killed before she can even speak at a trial.

In the most unlikely turn of events, an elf lord appears to her and offers her a choice: He will save her life and break her out of her prison, but only if she agrees to his terms. Blackthorn must work her healing abilities, offer her services to anyone who seeks her aid and, most importantly, he requires that she must renounce her plans for vengeance. Left without any other options, Blackthorn accepts these conditions, and her new life as a healer of the wood begins.

> ### AUTHOR'S NOTE
> This drink, a healing elixir, may not sate your thirst for revenge, but can help soothe the raging tempest within.

INGREDIENTS

- 2 oz gin
- 1 oz aloe juice
- ¾ oz lime juice
- ½ oz simple syrup
- 1 lime wheel

DIRECTIONS

1. In a shaker, combine the first 4 ingredients. Add ice and shake for 7 seconds.
2. Strain into a coupe and garnish with a lime wheel.

Ella's Choice

INSPIRED BY GAIL CARSON LEVINE'S **ELLA ENCHANTED**

Gail Carson Levine's *Ella Enchanted* is a reimagining of "Cinderella," with a particular twist: its heroine, Ella, must obey any order that she is given. As a babe, young Ella is visited by the fairy Lucinda, who bestowed upon Ella the gift of obedience—a powerful gift that, as Ella learns, can be used for good or for ill. Ella learns about the dark side of Lucinda's gift the hard way after her mother dies and Ella is sent to a boarding school. One of Ella's classmates, the vengeful Hattie, learns Ella obeys literally any command given to her...including the increasingly vile and cruel commands Hattie begins issuing. Just when things seem like they cannot get any worse, Ella's father (who has lost all of his fortune) remarries Dame Olga—Hattie's mother.

Thanks to another of Lucinda's gifts gone awry (the gift of eternal love between Ella's father and Dame Olga—even when Olga learns he is penniless and that she has been swindled), Ella becomes the target for all of her new stepmother's hatred.

Try as she might, despite all of her adventures and searches, it seems there's no hope for Ella as Lucinda cannot take back her gifts once given. The real danger rears its head when Olga and Hattie learn Ella has captured the heart of Prince Char. Knowing she would only be a liability to her beloved and to their kingdom should anyone learn of her curse, Ella cannot marry her Prince. But then a peculiar thing happens: When the greedy Olga commands Ella to marry Prince Char, Ella can finally—finally!—make her own choice and break the spell.

Sweet and effervescent, this drink captures the magic of Ella's own earnest free will.

> **AUTHOR'S NOTE**
>
> Nothing chases away bitterness better than sparkling wine and sorbet.

INGREDIENTS

- 1 **scoop strawberry sorbet**
- 1½ **oz aged rum**
- ½ **oz lemon juice**
- 2–3 **oz sparkling wine**
- 3 **strawberry slices**

DIRECTIONS

1. Place the scoop of sorbet into a coupe. Wait 2 minutes to allow the sorbet to begin melting.
2. Pour the rum and lemon juice on top, then slowly add the sparkling wine. Pour carefully, as the sorbet will activate the carbonation.
3. Garnish with strawberry slices and serve with a small spoon.

> **FROM THE BAR**
>
> To keep your drink nice and cold, be sure to chill the sparkling wine before adding it to the sorbet in step 2.

Red's Fireball

INSPIRED BY WIZARDS OF THE COAST'S
DUNGEONS & DRAGONS: PLAYER'S HANDBOOK

Perhaps one of the most ubiquitous (and certainly one of the most consistently damaging) spells in Dungeons & Dragons (5th Edition), *fireball* is the preferred spell of choice for sorcerers and wizards (as well as enterprising bards). In many a D&D campaign, there is always that one player who relies heavily on this highly damaging spell—it nearly always deals damage and consumes everything in its 20-foot-radius path. Does the player who casts *fireball* care there are allies and/or fellow players in the aforementioned radius? Does the player who casts *fireball* even ask how large the room is or what others in the party suggest?

Nay, the caster of *fireball* cares not for such petty matters! They just need to borrow a few more d6s.

This particular cinnamon-infused whiskey packs the same power as its namesake, with the bonus effect of inducing excitement, paucity of confidence and, ultimately, the thrill that comes from making terrible, but occasionally hilarious, decisions. Named for a tiefling member of a recently concluded campaign (thanks in part to their prolific producing of this spell), Red, this one's for you.

> **AUTHOR'S NOTE**
> Some players just want to watch the world burn.

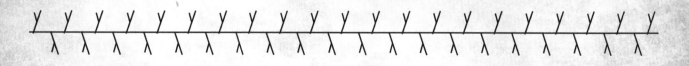

INGREDIENTS

- 2 oz cinnamon-infused whiskey (or premade cinnamon whiskey)
- ¾ oz pineapple juice
- ¾ oz lime juice
- ½ oz demerara syrup
- 1 cinnamon stick

DIRECTIONS

1. In a shaker, combine the first 4 ingredients with ice.
2. Shake for 7 seconds and strain into a lowball glass with fresh ice.
3. Garnish by lighting one end of the cinnamon stick on fire and placing it into the glass. Extinguish the flame before drinking.

FROM THE BAR

If you want your cinnamon whiskey to have a real kick, add 4 to 6 whole dried red chile peppers. Strain after infusing.

RED'S FIREBALL

CASTING TIME
1 action

RANGE
The entire bar and anyone within earshot

COMPONENTS
V, S, M (cinnamon, whiskey, infernal shot glass and a bit of trepidation, which the spell consumes)

SCHOOL
Delusion

You shout the command word ("Cheers!"), raising a glass and imbibing a spicy, warming liquor that consumes your inhibition and evokes within you the blazing passion of your hidden self. Each creature within a 30-foot radius must succeed on a Wisdom saving throw. On a failed save, they must join you in imbibing the same delicious beverage, falling under its spell and reveling in the chaos that follows enjoying something so good it should be unlawful.

Sectumsempra

INSPIRED BY J.K. ROWLING'S
HARRY POTTER AND THE HALF-BLOOD PRINCE

In the penultimate book in the *Harry Potter* series, Harry returns to a Hogwarts now blissfully free from evil bureaucrat Dolores Umbridge's clutches. This time around, Headmaster Albus Dumbledore has taken to heart the damage that happened by leaving Harry completely in the dark and has decided to bring the Boy Who Lived into his confidence by offering him private lessons to fight the Dark Lord. (After the events of *Harry Potter and the Order of the Phoenix*, Harry has finally heard the prophecy made about him and Voldemort and knows "neither can live while the other survives.")

While Harry deeply respects Dumbledore, he becomes frustrated (and quick to anger) when both the Headmaster and friends Hermione and Ron are reluctant to believe Harry's suspicion that something is wrong with Draco Malfoy, his longtime nemesis. So, Harry decides to take matters into his own hands, confronting Draco with a new spell he found scribbled in his Potions book: *Sectumsempra*.

With lasting horror, Harry learns firsthand why one should never use spells without explanation or instruction. The curse is no silly Jelly-Legs Jinx or hilarious Bat-Bogey Hex but a working of Dark magic that leaves Draco covered in deep, bloody gashes.

Like its namesake, this drink may look innocuous at first glance—but is not to be taken lightly.

> **AUTHOR'S NOTE**
> ....
> For enemies.
> Or good friends.

INGREDIENTS
- **2 oz light rum**
- **1 oz lime juice**
- **4 oz coconut water**
- **¾ oz grenadine**

DIRECTIONS
1. In a highball glass, stir together the first 3 ingredients.
2. Add ice into the glass, then measure out the grenadine in a separate shot glass.
3. Right before serving, slowly pour the grenadine into the highball glass so that it trickles down and sinks to the bottom. Add a straw to gently stir before sipping.

The Devoured Sin

INSPIRED BY TOCHI ONYEBUCHI'S *BEASTS MADE OF NIGHT*

Imagine a world where sins—every transgression, every lie, every nightmare—are real, tangible beasts. In Tochi Onyebuchi's *Beasts Made of Night*, sins can be extracted from the transgressor's body, transformed into inisisa (or sin-beasts), and their burden consumed by a select group of people, the aki (or sin-eaters). As you might guess, consuming sins comes at a high price for both the sinner (financial) and for the aki (spiritual). For each sin an aki consumes, a tattoo appears on his or her skin. The burden of that monster now lives within the aki, and as that psychic debt continues to pile up over each sin devoured, it can drive the eater mad.

While it might seem that aki should be celebrated members of this world, in fact, they are exploited by Mages—those who accept the money for inisisa, but who bear none of the consequences. Aki, on the other hand, are like slaves. They are feared, not just because of the tattoos that cover their bodies but also their inevitable madness.

> ### AUTHOR'S NOTE
> When Taj, the protagonist of *Beasts Made of Night*, describes consuming inisisa, it's an experience that burns with both heat and cold, cruel-edged and penetrating marrow-deep—not unlike certain types of amaro.

INGREDIENTS
- 1 oz rye whiskey
- 1½ oz amaro (e.g., Fernet Branca, Averna, Cynar or Jägermeister)
- 3 oz cola
- Grated nutmeg

DIRECTIONS
1. In a lowball glass, pour in the first 3 ingredients and add ice.
2. Garnish with grated nutmeg.

A NOTE ON AMARO

An Italian herbal liqueur first produced in monasteries in the 13th century, amaro (the Italian word for bitter) is a bittersweet infusion of grape brandy or wine and any number of botanical ingredients—including aromatic bark, citrus peels, flowers, herbs and spices—that's been sweetened with sugar syrup and left to age. Originally consumed as an after-dinner digestive aid (but by all means, don't let that stop you from enjoying it as an aperitif), amaro adds a complex aromatic note to virtually any beverage. Use it as you would bitters (sparingly) or incorporate it into your drink as a base. Granted, various brands are beloved by amaro aficionados for their closely guarded secret blends, so you'll want to shop around and test out a few samples to decide which combination of regional herbs bewitches your palate the most.

Faerie Fruit

INSPIRED BY HOLLY BLACK'S **THE CRUEL PRINCE**

Holly Black's *Cruel Prince* trilogy largely takes place in the realm of Faerie, a beautiful but brutal place for mere mortals. Jude Duarte is better prepared than most humans who dare enter Faerie thanks to her family history and her foster father, the redcap warlord Madoc. Jude and twin sister Taryn are full mortals—after their mother, Eva, ran away from Madoc, they were conceived and born into hiding in the human world. All was happy for Jude and her family until the vengeful Madoc discovered the truth of his wife's treachery and hunted down Eva and her human lover. But while Madoc is one of the fey and sworn to vengeance, he also is sworn to honor. Instead of killing Eva's human children, he raises them in Faerie.

Faerie fruit holds a powerful sway over mortals. Described as sweet and rotten at the same time, this forbidden fruit makes humans crave it to the point of starvation. In smaller doses, humans become pliant playthings for the inherently cruel fey.

> **AUTHOR'S NOTE**
> ....
> Suffice it to say,
> take it easy with this one:
> tasting forbidden fruit
> has consequences.

INGREDIENTS

- 5 oz red wine
- 1 oz crème de cassis
- 1 Tbsp blackberry jam
- ¾ oz lemon juice
- 3 dashes orange bitters
  Skewered fresh blackberries or
  a lemon wheel

DIRECTIONS

1. Combine the first 5 ingredients in a shaker without ice and shake for 3 seconds.
2. Add ice, then shake for 7 seconds.
3. Strain over fresh ice in a wine glass and garnish with either a skewer of blackberries or a lemon wheel.

Ged and Shadow

INSPIRED BY URSULA K. LE GUIN'S
THE EARTHSEA CYCLE

Ursula K. Le Guin's Earthsea is an ocean world counting thousands of different islands among its number. Across five novels and 11 short stories, Le Guin's *Earthsea Cycle* begins with *A Wizard of Earthsea* and follows an extraordinary and promising young man named Duny. When Duny's potential is discovered, he is taken as an apprentice by Ogion, a powerful and wise mage who teaches the younger man the importance of names—giving the apprentice his true name, Ged—and of balance. Ged, however, is ambitious and ultimately chooses to leave Ogion for a prodigious and renowned wizarding school.

It is at school on Roke Island that Ged tangles with magic beyond his abilities. Goading his rival into a duel, Ged attempts a spell that goes dangerously awry, summoning a dark shadow that costs the Archmage his life. The shadow creature may be temporarily banished by the Archmage's magic, but Ged soon learns that the creature has no name and will hunt him down to the ends of Earthsea.

Faced with the consequences of his actions, Ged turns to his old mentor, Ogion, for help. Following Ogion's advice, Ged finally confronts his shadow, knowing he must name it for any real peace.

> ### AUTHOR'S NOTE
> Heed Ogion's advice:
> You can't run away
> from your
> mistakes forever.

INGREDIENTS

- 1 **lemon slice**
  Black salt
- 2 **oz tequila or reposado tequila**
- ¾ **oz lemon juice**
- ¾ **oz vanilla syrup**
- 1 **egg white**

DIRECTIONS

1. Rub the lemon slice around the rim of a coupe glass, then dip the rim in black salt.
2. In a shaker without ice, combine the tequila, lemon juice, vanilla syrup and egg white and shake for 10 seconds.
3. Add ice, then shake again for 7 seconds. Strain into the coupe.

The Sorceress's Tea

INSPIRED BY PATRICIA A. MCKILLIP'S
OMBRIA IN SHADOW

Patricia A. McKillip's *Ombria in Shadow* is a lush, beautiful fantasy novel about two cities: Ombria, above ground, and the remains of an older, ghostly city beneath it. When Ombria's ruler dies suddenly, Domina Pearl seizes her opportunity. Declaring herself Queen Regent for her great-nephew, the young Prince Kyel, the powerful sorceress quickly dispenses of her enemies—including the dead king's longtime mistress Lydea and the king's bastard nephew Ducon Greve.

Thanks to a magical assistant named Mag, a girl made from wax by the great under-city sorceress Faey, Lydea is able to escape certain death. Desperate for help to save her city and Prince Kyel, Lydea turns to Faey for help against the "Black Pearl." She travels to the other city—the Shadow City—a place inhabited by ghosts and spirits whose channels and streets are known to few. But Faey's help is not easily won—she's a sorceress even more ancient than the long-lived Domina Pearl—though Lydea means to try with all her might. Upon meeting with Faey, Lydea is spellbound to drink an endless cup of tea, uttering the same phrases again and again until the enchantment is broken.

> **AUTHOR'S NOTE**
> ....
> Unless consumed in the
> Shadow City,
> this drink won't
> continue to refill itself.

INGREDIENTS

- 2 oz Earl Grey-infused gin
- ½ oz orange spice tea syrup
- 3 dashes orange bitters
- 1 orange peel

DIRECTIONS

1. Infuse gin with an Earl Grey tea bag for 15 minutes. Remove the tea bag and wring it out into the gin.
2. In a lowball glass, add infused gin, tea syrup and bitters. Add ice or 1 large ice cube and stir lightly to incorporate ingredients.
3. Garnish by expressing the oils of an orange peel over the top. Flame the peel if desired.

Shiori's Secret

INSPIRED BY ELIZABETH LIM'S **SIX CRIMSON CRANES**

Fairy tale retellings are rife with spells and curses, and such is true of Elizabeth Lim's *Six Crimson Cranes*. A reimagining of the Brothers Grimm fable "The Six Swans," Lim's version transports the tale to a pre-Silk Road Japanese- and Chinese-inspired world. The core of the original story (and its many permutations throughout Europe) is a king who remarries a beautiful woman of magical origin. The new queen enters the family and curses her seven stepchildren: six brothers are cursed to become swans and can only resume their human shapes for a brief period (usually, from dusk to dawn). The sister escapes and alone possesses the chance to break her family's curse—but to do so, she must not utter a single word until her task (usually to spin shirts out of fireweed/starflower/some kind of stinging nettle) is complete.

Lim's version of the tale remains true to the Grimm source material, with a beautiful stepmother who possesses great and terrible power and a young princess who alone possesses the ability to save her family and kingdom. The princess, Shiori, is headstrong and defiant of her family's wishes. She also has an innate ability to work magic, something she should not be able to do and must keep secret. It's a good thing that Shiori is used to keeping secrets because after she is cursed, speaking so much as a single word means her crane-ensorcelled brothers will die.

> **AUTHOR'S NOTE**
>
> For a good time, blend the flavors of this drink with Shiori's tight-lipped control.

MAKES 8 SERVINGS

INGREDIENTS
- 16 oz shochu
- 12 oz oolong tea
- 12 oz ginger beer
- 8 oz yuzu juice (or lemon juice)
- 6 oz demerara syrup
- Candied ginger

DIRECTIONS
1. In a bowl or pitcher, combine ingredients and add some ice. Stir lightly and then serve in lowball glasses with fresh ice.
2. Garnish with skewered candied ginger.

FROM THE BAR
To prepare in advance: Combine all ingredients except the ginger beer into a bowl or pitcher and refrigerate for up to 8 hours. Add in the ginger beer before serving.

The King of Scars

INSPIRED BY LEIGH BARDUGO'S *KING OF SCARS* DUOLOGY

One of the unassailably best characters from Leigh Bardugo's *Grishaverse* is Nikolai Lantsov. First introduced as Sturmhond—a loquacious and charming, if dangerous, pirate—his true identity is revealed as Prince Nikolai, second in line for the Ravkan throne. Thanks to his allegiance to Alina Starkov—a Grisha of the rarest order gifted with the ability to summon light—Nikolai makes a powerful enemy. The Darkling, a Grisha who can summon the darkness to Alina's light, curses the young prince and transforms him into a winged, fanged, human flesh-craving monster.

Through his bond with Alina, Nikolai is able to resist his monstrous urges and ultimately is saved and transformed back to human form when she kills the Darkling—but a small sliver of the Darkling's curse remains. Each night, Nikolai transforms back into the beast and feels the darkness within him grow. Now the King of Ravka, Nikolai's fate is dark and uncertain—and he knows that all of Ravka and his succession are in peril.

Nikolai is a fan favorite for many reasons. He knows when to quit and when to walk away from power—and that, dear reader, is the mark of a great leader.

AUTHOR'S NOTE

Heavy is the crown.

INGREDIENTS

- 2 oz aged rum
- 1 oz lime juice
- ¾ oz simple syrup
- 4–5 pieces of mint, torn in half
- 1 oz ginger beer
- 1 mint sprig

DIRECTIONS

1. Combine the first 4 ingredients into a shaker with ice.
2. Shake vigorously for 7 seconds, then strain into a highball glass with fresh ice.
3. Top with the ginger beer and lightly stir to incorporate. Garnish with a mint sprig.

Do What You Wish

INSPIRED BY MICHAEL ENDE'S
THE NEVERENDING STORY

The Neverending Story is probably best known by most people for either the 1984 film of the same name and/or the title song by Limahl. But, before the films (there are three, with diminishing returns), there was the book by Michael Ende. Originally written in German in 1979 and translated to English in 1983, the first film was (at the time) the most expensive ever produced outside of the United States as well as the most expensive German film ever made. Unless you have watched the first two films and read the book, you might not realize the first film actually only represents the first half of the novel. The second film—though starring different actors as the original's characters—rounds out the book's story.

One of the enduring themes in the films and book is that of sadness—there's Bastian, who has lost his mother and struggles with his relationship with his father; within the confines of the book-within-the-book/film, Atreyu loses his beloved horse, Artax, to the Swamps of Sadness; and a great Nothing threatens to consume all of Fantasia. The saddest thing in the second film and the second half of the book is, innocuously, wishes.

At the end of the first film/half of the book, the Childlike Empress gives Bastian AURYN (the intertwined ouroboros medallion). Bastian sees that AURYN has the words "Do What You Wish" engraved on the back, which he takes to heart. He keeps wishing for things, all of which are fulfilled magically, without realizing that each wish robs him of a memory. Bastian wishes for monsters and adventures to conquer, injuring Fantasia and even his friend, Atreyu—and by the end, Bastian forgets his mother, and then even his father, a testament to how getting everything you desire can come at a cursed cost.

> **AUTHOR'S NOTE**
> ....
> Every wish comes with a price. Make sure you are willing and able to pay it before wishing.

INGREDIENTS

- 2 oz your spirit of choice
- 1 oz honey syrup
- 1 oz lemon juice
- 1½ oz soda water
- Ground or freshly grated nutmeg

DIRECTIONS

1. In a shaker, combine the first 3 ingredients.
2. Shake vigorously for 7 seconds and strain into a highball glass with fresh ice. Top with soda water and lightly stir.
3. Garnish with nutmeg.

FANTASY DRINKING BUDDIES

The genre is loaded with charismatic characters who can spin a yarn over a pint or three. Here are a few we'd most like to raise a glass with.

Tyrion Lannister
George R.R. Martin's *A Song of Ice and Fire*

When determining who you want to share a drink with, there are a number of factors one can consider. Are they a good conversationalist? Do they have a bit of gossip or counsel to share? Are they willing to pick up the tab? With Tyrion Lannister, the quipping, cunning Halfman of the Lannister clan and one of George R.R. Martin's most beloved creations, one finds a figure for whom the answer to all those questions is yes. Whether you want to raise a glass with the architect of the great victory at the Battle of Blackwater, toast and boast with a man who's seen a dragon up close or simply hear that tale of the time he killed his father while the latter was on the john, as a drinking companion, Tyrion puts the imp in simply perfect.

Kvothe
Patrick Rothfuss's *The Name of the Wind*

Witty, outgoing and prone to spinning tales, Kvothe would be just the sort of drinking companion who could easily procure a few drinks on the house while regaling you, the barkeep and anyone within earshot about his previous exploits. A lute fanatic, there's a solid chance he'll belt out a few tunes to bring down the house and earn some coin (or perhaps create a distraction while you swipe another round). The guy's a seasoned scavenger, so expect him to have a few tricks up his sleeve as you venture off to the next venue on your bar crawl.

Geralt of Rivia
Andrzej Sapkowski's *The Witcher*

Who wouldn't want to pull up a stool next to this ivory-maned warrior? With his vast array of powerful potions, Geralt is something of a mixologist himself (he probably prefers the term "alchemist," but still), so you could convince him to enhance your boring brown ale with something a bit more magical. Instead of blacking out, you might actually be able to see clearly in the dark thanks to whatever concoction he creates. When you're done, don't forget to toss a coin to your witcher (and your bartender, for that matter).

Eliot Waugh
Lev Grossman's *The Magicians*

A hedonist doesn't just get the party started—they sustain it at all costs, which means Eliot's your huckleberry when it comes to having a fun-filled night of debauchery. Brakebills's unofficial mixologist (he created the Physical Kids' signature cocktail), Eliot is known to carry an enchanted flask that never empties. From drinking games to shameless karaoke, this brilliant bon vivant and charming musical theater nerd will keep you on the edge of your seat so long as you can keep his spirits up.

Temeraire
Naomi Novik's *Temeraire*

It's only fitting to have a hyper-intelligent dragon on this list. All the more so for those who tend to wax poetic after a few cocktails,

and considering Temeraire's broad reading list includes everything from Confucius to Newton to Goethe, he's a dragon of the Enlightenment with a wit as dazzling as his wings. This politically inclined powerhouse (did we mention he's also a weapon of war?) is the perfect sparring partner over stiff drinks, the sort of drinking companion who'll chat your ear off until last call. At which point you should politely ask him for a ride home.

Harry Dresden
Jim Butcher's *The Dresden Files*
If small talk makes your skin crawl, look no further than tossing back a few shots of the strong stuff with this supernatural private eye. A wizard for hire, Dresden's seen it all—from gnarly crime scenes (ever seen someone whose heart was ripped out?) to brushes with mob bosses, monster scorpions, werewolves, ectomancers, literal demons and more, he's got no shortage of paranormal adventures to mine for those who appreciate a morbid tale. He's also known to buy pizza in exchange for information, so be sure to hit up the "Za-Lord" when it's time to sober up.

Rubeus Hagrid
J.K. Rowling's *Harry Potter*
You know the towering half-giant's a big softie at heart, but anyone looking to pick a fight with you at the local watering hole will likely want to steer clear of the massive, wild-looking man wielding a pink umbrella. As Hogwarts's Keeper of Keys and Grounds, Gamekeeper and Care of Magical Creatures professor, Hagrid's led quite the colorful life and (with very little prompting) will likely be more than glad to open up about all the fantastic (read: dangerous) beasts he's encountered on his travels. Play your cards right and he might invite you back to his hut to meet his latest incendiary cross-breeding experiment. Then again, who needs liquid luck when you've got liquid courage?

Dream
Neil Gaiman's *The Sandman*
Arguably the second most powerful of the seven Endless siblings, Dream (aka Morpheus) is the sort of person who will understand you as far as you'd like to be understood. Like Jay Gatsby, he's a man for whom delusion and reality are one and the same—one man finds his tavern talks with Dream so fascinating that he meets up with Morpheus every century for a pint or two. With the power to make any dream a reality, you could count on him to throw one hell of a cocktail party if given the chance, and it sounds like he could really use the company. A word of warning: You'll want to dip before his sister Death shows up.

Merry, Pippin and Sam
J.R.R. Tolkien's *The Lord of the Rings*
When it comes to hospitality, it's hard to beat a Hobbit, and when it comes to Hobbits, it's hard to name any as enjoyable as Meriadoc Brandybuck, Peregrin Took and Samwise Gamgee (Frodo's great, too, he just always seems a little distant, or downright invisible). Whether it's a night out at the Prancing Pony or a pub crawl that leads all the way to Mordor, these three are clearly game for anything, especially if they can order potatoes. Pippin could sing a tune as we tuck into some fresh tomatoes, Merry might offer a toke or two of Old Toby and even when it seems we can't carry on any longer, Sam, our dear Sam, would offer to carry us.

Hoid, the King's Wit
Brandon Sanderson's *The Stormlight Archive*
Much like Tyrion Lannister, Hoid knows things, most notably because he's immortal and has put in the legwork to get his details right. A well-traveled storyteller with the ability to jump between worlds, he'll take your bar-hopping game to a whole new level. Since his day job consists of insulting people on behalf of the king in the most devastating way possible, you can guarantee he'll keep the laughs and drinks coming in equal measure. Just be sure to read the room, lest you make the wrong enemy.

CELEBRATIONS

These showstopping beverages are the
liquid centerpieces that will turn any
event into a grand gathering.

As You Wish

INSPIRED BY WILLIAM GOLDMAN'S *THE PRINCESS BRIDE*

Rob Reiner's *The Princess Bride* is a classic—a cornerstone of an entire generation's introduction to fantasy and an excellent adaptation of William Goldman's novel of the same name. Following a beautiful young woman named Buttercup and her beloved farm boy, Wesley, *The Princess Bride* is told through a framing narrative as a boy stays home sick in bed and his grandfather reads him a story. Though the grandson initially resists ("Is this a kissing book?"), he—along with the audience—is quickly swept away by the story of the morose Princess Buttercup, the Dread Pirate Roberts and the despicable Prince

Humperdink hunting them down.

Before he assumes the mantle of the Dread Pirate Roberts, the humble Wesley has an iconic, Buttercup-specific catchphrase: "As you wish." Of course, "As you wish" means much more than just acquiescence to Buttercup's requests and demands: She (and the audience) learn this oft-repeated phrase is Wesley's signature way of saying "I love you." And, more importantly, that Buttercup loves Wesley back. The farm boy-pirate saves the princess from a loveless marriage, she saves him from certain death and together they live happily ever after.

> ### AUTHOR'S NOTE
> True love—true reciprocated love—is the most powerful of elixirs. Even if you pronounce it "twoo wuv." And this recipe can be made "as you wish" with your choice of base spirit. Suggestions include vodka, gin, rum, whiskey, tequila or brandy.

INGREDIENTS

- 1½ oz alcohol of choice
- ½ triple sec
- ¾ oz lemon juice
- ½ oz honey syrup
- ¾ oz pomegranate juice
- 1 lemon peel

DIRECTIONS

1. Combine first 5 ingredients in a shaker with ice. Shake for 7 seconds and strain up into a coupe/martini glass or over fresh ice in a lowball glass.

2. Garnish by expressing the oils of the lemon peel over the top of the drink and then placing on the rim.

Goblet-Chilled Sangria

INSPIRED BY MAYA MOTAYNE'S
A FORGERY OF MAGIC SERIES

While he doesn't expect to become crown prince after the death of his brother, Alfie is no stranger to the finer elements that San Cristobal has to offer within the palace walls. Prince Alfie first takes to the palace libraries in order to find a way to bring his brother back via magical means, and when thwarted by the lack of answers, takes to the outer rim of the city (see Alfie's Spicy Hot Chocolate, pg. 16). A city of concentric circles, San Cristobal places its roughest and poorest citizens at the farthest circles (named the Pinch and the Bash)—in other words, places where Alfie doesn't quite fit in. But in the palace at the heart of the city? The newly appointed heir to the throne better know how to conduct himself.

In San Cristobal's finest royal celebrations, the aristocracy mingles while servants pass around elegant trays of canapés and beverages. The hero of these beverages is the noble sangria: a chilled, fruited concoction worthy of a king, courtier or anyone with a curious palate.

AUTHOR'S NOTE

To ensure the highest possible quality with your sangria, use fresh fruit that's in season for the royal treatment.

> MAKES 8 SERVINGS

INGREDIENTS

- 1 (750-ml bottle) **red wine**
- 5 oz **brandy (grape-based preferred)**
- 2½ oz **lemon juice**
- 2½ oz **fresh orange juice**
- 5 oz **demerara syrup**
- 1 **apple, diced**
- ⅓ cup **almonds**
- 20–25 **grapes**
- 8 **strawberries, sliced**

DIRECTIONS

1. In a pitcher, combine ingredients and stir. Refrigerate for 4 to 6 hours to mull together.
2. When ready to serve, pour the mixture into wine glasses with fresh ice. Garnish with a scoop of the sangria-soaked fruit and nuts in the glass.

FROM THE BAR

Demerara syrup is a 1:1 ratio of demerara sugar, a minimally processed sugarcane product with a light molasses flavor, and water. If you don't have any on hand, turbinado sugar or light brown sugar works.

Cold Fizzy
Strawberry Cordial

INSPIRED BY BRIAN JACQUES'S **REDWALL**

Brian Jacques's *Redwall* series is simultaneously insightful and delightful from both a story and culinary perspective—there are few descriptions of food and drink in fantasy novels that come close to Jacques's depictions in the world of Redwall.

Over the course of the 22-book series, readers follow the adventures of different woodland creatures who live in Mossflower Woods and of course the titular Redwall Abbey. Each of these anthropomorphic mice, rabbits and the like protects their homeland from vermin, and in the meantime, they dine very well. One of the most ubiquitous beverages in all of Redwall and Mossflower Woods is the strawberry cordial. Served at almost every important meal, most notably Nameday celebrations (which tend to be more formal and full of decadent delicacies), this is a sweet, cool, fizzy drink that is loved by Dibbuns (younglings) and adults alike.

> **AUTHOR'S NOTE**
>
> The strawberry cordial can easily be made alcoholic or non-alcoholic. Better yet, make two large batches (one for you, one for them) for maximum enjoyment.

INGREDIENTS

- 1½ oz strawberry syrup
- ½ oz lemon juice
- 4 oz sparkling wine or sparkling water
- 1 strawberry

DIRECTIONS

1. In a highball glass, build the contents of the cocktail without ice. Lightly stir and then slowly add ice.

2. Garnish with a strawberry on the rim.

The Rains of Castamere

INSPIRED BY GEORGE R.R. MARTIN'S **A SONG OF ICE AND FIRE**

There are many wedding celebrations in the canon of fantasy literature. Some are opulent, joyful affairs; some are practical, terse mergers born of political convenience or necessity. Others, arguably the least happy of all, get a little stabby. George R.R. Martin's *Song of Ice and Fire* world focuses largely on this last bucket of marital felicity.

As the ultimate example, take the union of Robb Stark to Talisa Maegyr and the subsequent fallout. In *A Clash of Kings*, the Seven Kingdoms are fractured after Robert Baratheon's death, creating an opportunity for five would-be kings: Joffrey Baratheon (Robert's eldest son with Cersei Lannister), Stannis Baratheon (the elder of Robert's brothers), Renly Baratheon (the younger of Robert's brothers), Robb Stark (King in the North) and Balon Greyjoy (Lord of the Iron Islands). During the course of the war, Robb

meets, falls in love with, marries and impregnates Talisa, a healer on the battlefield, thereby breaking a marriage pact between the Starks and the Freys—a slight that Walder Frey doesn't take lightly.

And yet, Walder seems appeased by having one of his daughters marry Edmure Tully (of Catelyn Stark's family line) as recompense. Walder extends hospitality and guest rights to the Starks for the wedding, and all seems repaired between the North and the Riverlands... until "The Rains of Castamere" starts to play.

Catelyn recognizes the song—the destruction of House Reyne of Castamere at the hands of Tywin Lannister— and watches in horror as her family and army are slaughtered at the hands of the treacherous House Frey and House Bolton, who've allied themselves with the Lannisters in support of Joffrey Baratheon (who, it's pretty clear, is a Lannister through and through).

AUTHOR'S NOTE

May be served to friends or enemies, but the author does not recommend breaking the law of guest in the vein of the Freys and Boltons.

> MAKES 12 SERVINGS

INGREDIENTS

- 25 oz (1 750-ml bottle) **sparkling wine**
- 10 oz **white tea**
- 10 oz **gin**
- 5 oz **white port**
- 50 oz **lemonade**
  Lemon wheels
  Large cherry syrup ice cubes or ice ring

DIRECTIONS

Combine all ingredients in a punch bowl with the ice. Lightly stir and serve in highball or lowball glasses.

FROM THE BAR

Made from white grapes grown in the Douro Valley of Portugal, white port has notes of apricots, green apples, peaches and unripe pears. Despite this fruity profile, it's typically drier than its red counterpart.

Graduation Day

INSPIRED BY NAOMI NOVIK'S **THE SCHOLOMANCE** SERIES

Naomi Novik's *Scholomance* series follows a group of young adults—children, really—who are whisked away to a magical school to learn their craft. The Scholomance isn't really like Hogwarts (see Butterbeer, pg. 56), nor is it much like the edgier Brakebills College for Magical Pedagogy (see Fillory and Further, pg. 31). Instead, it's an interdimensional magical school from which students get no reprieve from malevolent monsters who aim to kill all of the delicious young magical humans inside.

Within the Scholomance itself and in the larger version of the human world of Novik's imagining, magic is transactional—you must pay up in order to wield magical power. Traditionally, "good" magic is paid for with mana, which can be generated by doing arduous tasks that generally require some type of effort and concentration (sit-ups, jumping jacks or knitting, for example). The dark path of magic is paid for with malia, which uses the energy force from other living things.

At the Scholomance, students band together to share mana, form alliances to extract mana from others and, in some rare instances, just take the dark path and wield malia. No matter how close you might be to other students or what alliances you've formed, at the end of the day, every student in a graduating class needs to make a mad dash to the exit and avoid being eaten. In other words, the Scholomance is essentially an "every person for themselves" situation. The lucky survivors are able to escape the Scholomance and perhaps even enjoy this libation as a rite of passage.

> **AUTHOR'S NOTE**
>
> In true high school graduation fashion, this large batch punch can be served non-alcoholic (aka the "mana" version), or spiked with harder-to-sniff-out vodka (aka the "malia" version).

MAKES 10 SERVINGS

INGREDIENTS

- 8 oz cranberry syrup
- 15 oz lemonade
- 20 oz ginger ale
- 10 oz lemon juice
  Sherbet ring (Mix equal parts lemonade and raspberry sherbet and freeze in a ring mold overnight)
- 15 oz vodka, optional

DIRECTIONS

1. Combine ingredients in a punch bowl, then add the sherbet ring.
2. Mix lightly to combine and ladle into serving cups.

FROM THE BAR

Unlike its dairy-free cousin, sorbet, sherbet is a fruit-flavored frozen dessert made with milk, cream and egg white or gelatin. When dumped into ginger ale or other carbonated beverages, it chills the drink and creates a delicious technicolor fizz.

The High King's Coronation

INSPIRED BY HOLLY BLACK'S **THE CRUEL PRINCE**

In the dramatic events ending Holly Black's *The Cruel Prince*, the elder High King of Faerie is released from his throne with a plan to coronate his third-born son, Dain, in his place. However, a good amount of treachery occurs, with the firstborn son, Balekin, murdering his father and sisters on the spot. Faerie, as it turns out, features the same cutthroat Machiavellian politics as the human realm.

Witness to this mayhem is Jude Duarte, a human girl who resides in Faerie with her twin sister Taryn and her faerie siblings Vivi and Oak. Jude watches in horror as she pieces together the truth: her father (in spirit, if not in blood) Madoc is in cahoots with the usurper Balekin for Madoc's own personal gain. Jude knows Madoc's true desire is to control the throne, which he can do if his own adopted son Oak receives the crown. Acting with speed, cunning and a dash of recklessness, Jude hatches her own counterplan to save her infant brother by placing her puppet on the throne. These machinations all hinge on a delicate and poisonous drink, served to Madoc and Jude's opponents as part of the ceremonial toast.

> **AUTHOR'S NOTE**
> ....
> Never, ever drink a coronation toast. It never goes well.

INGREDIENTS
- 1 **Tbsp blackberry jam**
- ¾ **oz lime juice**
- 1½ **oz aged rum**
- 1½ **oz sparkling wine**
- 1 **blackberry**

DIRECTIONS
1. Combine first 3 ingredients in a shaker with ice. Shake vigorously for 7 seconds and strain up into a flute or coupe.
2. Top with sparkling wine and float a blackberry in the drink.

Princess Ozma's Lacasa

INSPIRED BY L. FRANK BAUM'S **THE ROAD TO OZ**

In *The Wonderful Wizard of Oz*, Kansas native Dorothy Gale is swept away in a tornado and transported to a magical realm with witches (both good and wicked), magical companions, emerald cities and ruby slippers. Many readers are familiar with the tale of the yellow brick road to find the Wizard of Oz, but fewer are familiar with the other books in the *Oz* series. Similarly, while Dorothy is the best-known heroine of Oz, Princess Ozma is the rightful and immortal ruler of Baum's magical fairyland. Ozma appears in every book in the series except the first. She's described as a beautiful young woman, a fair ruler and an integral part of Oz's operations. She also throws a mean party.

In *The Road to Oz*, Dorothy and her dog, Toto, are transported back to Oz on another adventure, where they try to help new friends procure invitations to Princess Ozma's lavish birthday bash. After many adventures, introductions to several new characters and chance meetings with the inhabitants of Oz, Dorothy manages to make it to the party with most of her new friends. Here, Dorothy and Ozma become fast best friends, while sharing a drink that is described as sweeter and nicer than soda water or lemonade.

INGREDIENTS

- 4 oz hibiscus tea
- ½ oz lime juice
- 1 oz pomegranate juice
- ¾ honey syrup
- Pomegranate seeds

DIRECTIONS

1. Combine first 4 ingredients in a shaker with ice. Shake for 7 seconds and strain into a wine glass with ice.

2. Garnish with pomegranate seeds.

The Court of Iorek Byrnison

INSPIRED BY PHILIP PULLMAN'S *HIS DARK MATERIALS*

His Dark Materials follows the inter-dimensional adventures of Lyra Belacqua, an orphan raised at Jordan College in an alternate version of Oxford. Desperate to save her best friend Roger from the Gobblers (a shadowy group of children snatchers), Lyra runs away from Mrs. Coulter (for more on this piece of work, see The Coulter, pg. 39). Along the way, she meets Gyptians, witches, aeronauts and talking polar bears, the latter being very important and central characters, especially in *The Golden Compass*.

Iorek Byrnison is a panserbjørne: one of the great armored bears, fierce warriors with formidable strength and intelligence. But Iorek is no ordinary panserbjørne; he was the king of Svalbard, tricked out of his throne by treachery from his usurper, Iofur Raknison, who killed a challenger in a fight. Exiled, and with his armor stolen (which, to a panserbjørne, is their soul), Iorek is befriended by Lyra, who promises to get him his armor—and in the process earns her name, Silvertongue, for her loquacious and cunning way with words.

Lyra Silvertongue talks her way into more than just Iorek's good graces in *The Golden Compass*; she also helps her friend reclaim his throne by tricking Iofur into a battle for rule of the panserbjørne.

AUTHOR'S NOTE

After besting a usurper and reclaiming one's throne, the author recommends this panserbjørne-approved large batch celebratory drink.

INGREDIENTS

- 4 oz white wine
- ¾ oz lemon juice
- 2 oz white cranberry juice
- ½ oz honey syrup
- 1 lemon peel

DIRECTIONS

1. Combine first 4 ingredients in a blender with a cup of ice. Blend for 10 to 15 seconds until incorporated.

2. Pour into a wine glass and garnish with a lemon peel.

Glossary

YOUR GUIDE TO ESSENTIAL COCKTAIL INGREDIENTS AND BASIC RECIPES.

BASE SPIRITS

Brandy
A spirit distilled from wine or fruit juice. Some brandies from specific regions of the world (Armagnac, Calvados, Cognac) are named for where they were produced, while others (applejack, for example) are named after the fruit source.

Calvados
An apple brandy from the Normandy region of France. Calvados can only be produced in this specific area; otherwise, it's called apple brandy or applejack (in the U.S.).

Gin
A juniper and botanical distilled spirit ranging on average in proof level between 35 percent to 55 percent ABV. While gin can use any botanicals and ingredients, it must have juniper as the base botanical. Gin originated in Europe and is one of the most popular spirits in the world.

Mezcal
A distilled spirit between 40 percent and 55 percent ABV that is made exclusively in Mexico from any type of agave plant. Before popular worldwide enjoyment, mezcal has traditionally been used for ceremonial, religious and celebratory moments in Mexican culture. The majority of mezcal is produced in the state of Oaxaca, but is currently made throughout the country.

Tequila
A Mexican distillate made entirely from the blue Weber agave plant, tequila is produced by cooking the heart of the agave plant and crushing down the fibers to release the sugars and allowing them to ferment before distillation. Tequila can be rested and aged in barrels and comes in reposado (aged up to one year), añejo (one to two years) and extra añejo (three years or more).

Rum
A distillate made of sugarcane that is turned into either molasses or juice. Produced worldwide, but most commonly found in the Caribbean and Central and South America, the proof level of rum can be between 40 percent and 80 percent ABV. Most rum is aged in barrels, including white rum, which often is filtered after the aging process.

Vodka
Pure vodka is a clear, colorless and often neutral spirit that has a minimum proof of 40 percent ABV in the U.S. and 37.5 percent ABV in Europe and other parts of the world. The base of the spirit can be made from any ingredient and is most traditionally derived from grains (corn, wheat, rye), potatoes and fruits. In the modern era vodka is also being made from milk, honey, sugarcane and other fermentable food sources.

Whiskey
A spirit distilled from grains—typically rye, barley or corn—then aged in oak barrels. Certain whiskeys (scotch or bourbon, for example) have specific requirements in order to earn a designation beyond "whiskey." Some countries drop the e.

Scotch (Peated, Blended)
Produced in Scotland, this whisky is best known for being made from malted barley (also grain) and can be very distinct based upon the regionality of the distillate. All scotches are aged for a minimum of 3 years in oak barrels. As of now, there are more than 141 distilleries in production throughout Scotland. Blended scotches source scotch from various distilleries (or within their own) to blend together. Peated scotches use peat as a heat source when malting the barley. This process produces a smoky aroma that stays in the grain and then transfers to the bottle, giving the scotch a unique flavor.

LIQUEURS & FORTIFIED WINES

Amaro
A bittersweet, lower-proof liqueur originally made in Italy and considered a digestif (an after-dinner digestive beverage). Typically made with herbs, spices and fruits, there are hundreds of amari produced worldwide, each with its own unique flavor profile.

Chartreuse
A French herbal liqueur made by two Carthusian monks from a secret recipe, this overproof spirit is naturally green. The yellow variety, introduced almost 100 years after the original, is lower in proof, sweeter and uses a different composition of herbs.

Crème de Cacao
A chocolate liqueur that is usually brown or white. For the recipes in this book, we recommend the white varietal for aesthetic reasons.

Crème de Violette
A violet-flavored liqueur originally made in the 19th century. It's lower-proof, floral, sweet and used in classic cocktails such as the aviation.

Pimento Dram
An allspice liqueur typically made with a rum base, sugar and allspice/pimento berries.

Pimm's
An English, gin-based liqueur that's low proof and has citrus and spice notes. Created in 1823, this drink is most frequently used in a Pimm's Cup.

Ports, Sherries and Vermouths
These are aromatized and fortified wines, meaning small amounts of higher-proof alcohol have been added to them to help make them more shelf-stable. Refrigerate them after opening. Ports will last from one week to two months, sherries for one week and vermouths for three months.

Manzanilla Sherry
Made in Cadiz, Spain, the aroma of this pale dry wine is reminiscent of chamomile (or manzanilla, which is the Spanish translation). This fortified wine has a bit of salinity and savoriness due to its production by the sea.

White Port
A Portuguese fortified wine made from white grape varietals, the palate can run from dry to sweet. We suggest using dry options for the cocktails in this book.

Triple Sec
A sweet, orange-flavored liqueur that originated in France and ranges in proof level from 17 percent to 40 percent ABV. Typically clear, triple sec is often used as a modifier in classic cocktails. High quality triple secs at the 40 percent ABV level are recommended for the cocktails in this book.

ADDITIONAL INGREDIENTS
Bitters
Best thought of as seasoning for your cocktails, creating layers of additional flavor, bitters are made using high-proof, neutral grain alcohol infused with botanicals and bittering ingredients. They are shelf stable. Only use a few drops (aka dashes) to impart their flavors.

Butterfly Pea Flowers
Native to Asia, these flowers have a brilliant, naturally deep blue color that can be extracted when dried. Commonly used as a tea, it has a light floral flavor. It changes color when mixed with citrus.

Edible Shimmer Dust
This dust is 100 percent FDA-approved and can be easily purchased online or in most specialty cake decorating shops to add a little sparkle to food and drink. DO NOT use craft glitter or shimmer.

Egg White
Used as a texturizer mostly to create the foam layer on the top of a shaken cocktail, egg white can help cut the acidity of a drink and dries it out (so it's not as sweet). They can only be used in shaken drinks, not stirred. When working with egg whites, crack them in a separate container before adding them to your shaker to ensure no yolks or shells end up in the drink.

Ginseng
The root of plants from the genus *Panax*, ginseng has been used for centuries in traditional medicine and is widely popular in Korean and Chinese cooking.

Goldenrod Tea
This tea has a slight anise-like flavor. We recommend using store-bought goldenrod.

Green Spirulina
An algae that's vibrant green due to its high levels of chlorophyll, this superfood is rich in vitamins and minerals.

Grenadine
A cocktail bar staple, this nonalcoholic syrup is made from pomegranate and a splash of orange blossom water.

Kukicha (Twig) Tea
Also known as bōcha, this Japanese tea is made from the stalks, stems and twigs separated from green tea leaves during production.

Maple Syrup
Use grade A or B maple syrup for your drinks. Beware of "maple syrup" that is merely corn syrup with flavors and additives.

Mead
A popular beverage in ancient and medieval periods, mead is made by fermenting honey.

Milk
Any recipe using milk can also be made with alternative milk, such as oat, coconut, almond, pistachio, soy and more. We suggest using unsweetened varieties to ensure balance in your drinks.

Shochu
A distilled beverage originating in Japan and typically made from sweet potatoes, barley, rice, buckwheat or brown sugar, the ABV tends to hover between 25 and 35 percent.

SYRUPS

Each syrup can be refrigerated for up to 2 to 3 weeks.

Ale Syrup
In a saucepan on low heat, combine 1 cup ale and 1 cup sugar. Stir until the sugar dissolves and the carbonation subsides, then let cool. Using a golden ale or a pale ale is recommended if you would like a slight hint of bitterness.

Butter Syrup
In a saucepan on low heat, combine 1½ cups brown sugar and 1 cup water. Once the sugar is dissolved, add ¾ cup (6 oz) of salted butter and stir until well incorporated. Remove from heat and let cool.

Chai Syrup
Boil 1 cup of water and allow 1 chai tea bag to steep for 10 minutes. Remove the tea bag and mix in 1 cup of sugar. Mix until the sugar dissolves and let cool.

Cherry Syrup
Combine 1 cup of either pitted or frozen cherries with 1 cup of water and 1 cup of sugar in a blender. Blend on high for 1 minute. Strain with a fine mesh strainer or cheesecloth.

Cherry Syrup Ice Ring
Your ice ring should be a 2:1 ratio of water to cherry syrup. Take the volume of your ice ring mold (a bundt pan will do), divide into thirds and measure out ⅓ cherry syrup and the rest water. Combine in the mold and freeze 24 hours. To make cherry syrup ice cubes, pour the syrup into ice cube molds and freeze overnight.

Cranberry Syrup
Boil 2 cups of water with 1 cup of cranberries for 15 minutes. Reduce heat and add 1½ cups sugar. Mix and allow to dissolve. Strain to remove the cranberries.

Coconut Water Syrup
Combine 1 cup of coconut water with 1 cup of sugar. Stir until dissolved. Note: If your coconut water is relatively sweet, use ¾ cup sugar.

Demerara Syrup
Combine 1 cup of warm water with 1 cup of demerara sugar. Stir until dissolved.

Green Tea Syrup
Boil 1 cup of water, add 1 green tea bag and let steep for 15 minutes. Remove the tea bag and add 1 cup of sugar. Stir until dissolved.

Grenadine
Combine 1 cup pomegranate juice with 1 cup of sugar and 2 drops of orange blossom water. Stir until the sugar dissolves (if sugar won't dissolve, you can warm the pomegranate juice and sugar in a saucepan on the stove).

Honey Syrup
Combine 1 cup of warm water with 1 cup of honey. Stir until dissolved.

Mint Syrup
Blanche the mint by placing it in boiling water for about 10 seconds, then take it out and submerge it into a bowl of water with ice for a minute. Remove and pat dry. Combine ¼ cup of mint leaves, 1 cup of water and 1 cup of sugar in a blender. Blend for 1 minute and let sit for 5 minutes. Strain to remove any stems or bits.

Orange Spice Tea Syrup
Heat 1 cup of water with 1 orange spice tea bag for 15 minutes and allow the tea to steep. Discard the tea bag and add 1 cup of sugar. Stir until dissolved.

Poppy Seed Syrup
In a pan on low heat, lightly toast 1 Tbsp poppy seeds for 5 minutes. Be sure to move them around the pan to avoid burning. Remove from the stovetop, then place into a mortar and crush with a pestle to a fine consistency. You can also use a spice grinder. In a saucepan on medium heat, combine the crushed seeds with 1 cup water and 1 cup of sugar and stir until the sugar dissolves. Reduce heat to low and let sit for 10 minutes. Remove from heat and let cool.

Safflower Syrup
Boil 2 cups of water with 2 Tbsp of dried safflower for 15 minutes. Reduce heat and let cool for 10 minutes. Measure 1 cup of the safflower steeped water, mix with 1 cup of sugar and stir until dissolved.

Simple Syrup
Combine 1 cup of warm water with 1 cup of sugar. Stir until dissolved.

Strawberry Syrup
Combine 1 cup of sliced strawberries with 1 cup of water and 1 cup of sugar in a blender. Blend on high for 1 minute. Strain.

Vanilla Syrup
Slice 1 vanilla bean and scrape the insides into a pot with 2 cups of water. Add the pod and bring the water to a boil. Allow it to boil for 15 minutes, remove from heat and let sit 10 minutes. Add 1½ cups of sugar and mix until dissolved. Pour the syrup (with the vanilla bean for added flavor) into a jar or container.

INFUSIONS

Infusions enhance a spirit or other ingredient and add an additional layer of flavor to a drink.

Apple-Infused Whiskey
Cut half of an apple into slices. Place the slices into a mason jar, then add 8 oz of whiskey. Seal and allow it to sit at room temperature for a minimum of 48 hours. If possible, agitate or lightly shake the jar every 12 hours. The apple slices can be used for garnish, baking or eating.

Black Tea-Infused Rye
Add 8 oz of rye whiskey into a jar or container with 1 black tea bag and allow it to steep for 15 minutes. Remove and wring out the tea bag.

Butterfly Pea Flower-Infused Gin
Combine 1 Tbsp dried butterfly pea flowers (or 1 tea bag) and 8 oz gin in a mason jar and let steep for 20 minutes. Strain flowers or remove tea bag.

Cherry-Infused Rum
Combine ¼ cup pitted cherries with 8 oz rum in a mason jar. Seal and allow it to sit for a minimum of 24 hours. Agitate or lightly shake every 12 hours. Remove the cherries (can be used for garnish or to eat).

Chinese Five Spice-Infused Sweet Vermouth
Combine ½ Tbsp Chinese five spice powder with 8 oz sweet vermouth in a mason jar. Allow it to sit for 24 hours and agitate or shake it every 4 to 6 hours. Finely strain the mixture with double cheesecloth to remove the powder.

Cinnamon-Infused Whiskey
Combine 2 cinnamon sticks with 8 oz of whiskey in a mason jar. Seal and allow to sit at room temperature for a minimum of 48 hours. If possible, agitate or lightly shake the jar every 12 hours.

Earl Grey-Infused Gin
Combine 1 Earl Grey tea bag with 8 oz of gin in a mason jar. Seal and allow it to steep for 20 minutes. Remove tea bag.

Goldenrod Tea-Infused Vodka
Combine 1 tea bag or 1 Tbsp of goldenrod tea with 8 oz of vodka in a mason jar. Seal and allow to steep for 20 minutes. Strain or remove tea bag.

Herb-Infused Olive Oil
In a pan on low heat, combine 4 oz olive oil with 1 rosemary sprig. Cook for 3 to 4 minutes. Remove from heat and let cool. Discard the rosemary and pour the oil into a jar, then add 4 oz additional olive oil. Keep the oil in the fridge and use within 1 week.

Rooibos-Infused Gin
Combine 1 tea bag or 1 Tbsp of rooibos tea with 8 oz of gin in a mason jar. Seal and allow it to steep for 20 minutes. Strain or remove tea bag.

Rose Hip-Infused Vodka
Combine 1 Tbsp dried rose hips or 1 rose hip tea bag with 8 oz of vodka in a mason jar. Seal and allow it to steep for 30 minutes. Strain or remove tea bag.

Rosemary-Infused Gin
Combine 2 sprigs of rosemary with 8 oz of gin in a mason jar. Seal and allow to sit at room temperature for a minimum of 48 hours. If possible, agitate or lightly shake the jar every 12 hours. Strain infusion with a fine strainer before using.

Strawberry-Infused Gin
Combine ½ cup sliced strawberries with 12 oz gin in a mason jar. Allow to sit for a minimum of 24 hours. Strain before serving.

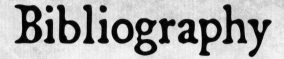

Bibliography

This book features recipes inspired by dozens of classic and contemporary fantasy works. If you're thirsty for more adventure, presented below are the referenced works—each of which is an enjoyable experience in its own right (but can be incrementally improved when paired with one of the recipes in this collection). Cheers!

SERIES

Beasts Made of Night by Tochi Onyebuchi
1. *Beasts Made of Night* (2017)
2. *Crown of Thunder* (2018)
The Devoured Sin .... pg. 109

Blackthorn & Grim by Juliet Marillier
1. *Dreamer's Pool* (2014)
2. *Tower of Thorns* (2015)
3. *Den of Wolves* (2016)
Blackthorn's Bargain .... pg. 104

The Books of Ambha by Tasha Suri
1. *Empire of Sand* (2018)
2. *Realm of Ash* (2019)
Rose Sharbat .... pg. 70

The Chronicles of Narnia by C.S. Lewis
1. *The Lion, the Witch and the Wardrobe* (1950)
2. *Prince Caspian* (1951)
3. *The Voyage of the Dawn Treader* (1952)
4. *The Silver Chair* (1953)
5. *The Horse and His Boy* (1954)
6. *The Magician's Nephew* (1955)
7. *The Last Battle* (1956)
Edmund's Temptation .... pg. 76
Jadis (The White Witch) .... pg. 71
Lucy's Cordial .... pg. 91

A Court of Thorns and Roses by Sarah J. Maas
1. *A Court of Thorns and Roses* (2015)
2. *A Court of Mist and Fury* (2016)
3. *A Court of Wings and Ruin* (2017)
4. *A Court of Frost and Starlight* (2018)
5. *A Court of Silver Flames* (2021)
The Huntress (Feyre) .... pg. 69
The Night Court (Rhysand) .... pg. 81
The Spring King (Tamlin) .... pg. 75

The Dark Star Trilogy by Marlon James
1. *Black Leopard, Red Wolf* (2019)
2. *Moon Witch, Spider King* (2022)
The Red Wolf .... pg. 44

The Dark Tower by Stephen King
1. *The Gunslinger* (1982)
2. *The Drawing of the Three* (1987)
3. *The Waste Lands* (1991)
4. *Wizard and Glass* (1997)
5. *The Little Sisters of Eluria* (1998)
6. *Wolves of the Calla* (2003)
7. *Song of Susannah* (2004)
8. *The Dark Tower* (2004)
9. *The Wind Through the Keyhole* (2012)
The Fall of Gilead .... pg. 78

Discworld by Terry Pratchett
NOTE: There are 41 titles in this expansive series, but for ease of reference, we're listing the 10th below.
10. *Moving Pictures* (1990)
Dried Frog Pills .... pg. 95

The Dragonriders of Pern by Anne McCaffrey
NOTE: The Pern *series is far-ranging and includes many different works. This recipe draws exclusively from the original trilogy and the nested* Harper Hall *Trilogy. It is recommended to read the* Harper Hall *Trilogy before reading* The White Dragon *(Original Trilogy, Book 3).*
The Harper Hall Trilogy:
1. *Dragonsong* (1976)
2. *Dragonsinger* (1977)
3. *Dragondrums* (1979)
The Original Trilogy:
1. *Dragonflight* (1968)
2. *Dragonquest* (1970)
3. *The White Dragon* (1978)
Pernese Klah .... pg. 52

The Dreamblood Duology by N.K. Jemisin
1. *The Killing Moon* (2012)
2. *The Shadowed Sun* (2012)
The Dreamblood .... pg. 27

Index

Acknowledgments

THEA JAMES

THERE ARE A LOT OF PEOPLE who come together to make a book, and this one is no exception. To the amazing team at Media Lab books, thank you for your vision, guidance and for keeping us all on track. In particular, thank you to Jeff Ashworth for lending your humor and editorial touch; to Juliana Sharaf for your endless patience and precision; to Courtney Kerrigan for your exceptional organization and operational prowess; to Mikio Sakai and Susan Dazzo for your artistic and design mastery; and to Phil Sexton for being the mastermind behind it all.

I am eternally grateful for Tim Foley's incredible artwork—there is no one else who can draw a tiefling casting a fireball while throwing back a shot and make it look artistic and cool.

This book would be nothing without Pam Wiznitzer, the real brains behind the story. Thank you, Pam, for your willingness to experiment, your creativity and your energy. Your recipes are true to the source material in ingenious ways, not to mention delicious, and I'm so grateful to have had the chance to partner on this book with you.

To all of the authors and worlds that inspired *Drinking With Wizards, Warriors and Dragons*: I raise my glass to you. I've said it before and I'll say it again, these books are my love letter to the wonders that you have created with your stories. Thank you for lending your magic to our mundane world.

To Ben Kolansky, my husband and my rock. Thanks for listening to me babble, for the repeat viewings of *Lord of the Rings* (it helps me write!) and for your feedback. You're the best, and I love you.

To the fellow fantasy nerd who is reading these words right now—this book is just as much for you as it is for me. Thank you for sharing your love for SFF, and I hope you enjoy these libations as much as I do.

PAMELA WIZNITZER

BEING A PART OF THIS EXPERIENCE has been nothing short of magical. There are countless people to thank for their support, excitement and patience, all of whom helped me bring my love of cocktails to life on the page.

Thanks to Media Lab Books, especially Jeff Ashworth, Courtney Kerrigan, Juliana Sharaf and Phil Sexton, for your guidance throughout this process. I appreciate all the time and expertise you've contributed along the way, especially your genuine excitement, intel and attention to detail. Working with a team like yours has been a dream and I am so grateful that my first publishing opportunity has been with all of you. Thank you for your stellar work.

To Thea James, the heartbeat of this project and a true visionary. Your knowledge of this genre is beyond inspiring and your passion brings each of the stories and characters to life. I cannot thank you enough for trusting me with this project and letting me shake and stir alongside your brilliance. It's an honor.

To Leah Doyle, my magical mermaid muse and the ultimate connector who made this a reality. Thank you for being my biggest cheerleader and for always believing in me.

To my tribe and friends (you know who you all are), your constant support and love invigorates me daily.

My family, Josh, Nathaniel and Mom for letting me take the road less traveled years ago, embracing my dream to "be a bartender." And to Dad, the ultimate fantasy fanatic who explained to me the world of hobbits, wizards, dragons and more from a young age. I hope these drinks make you proud.

Finally, to my younger self, the little girl who would secretly crawl to check the back of her closet nightly, believing that perhaps this time she would discover the entrance to Narnia. This is for you.

About the Authors

THEA JAMES is the author of *Drinking With Wizards, Warriors and Dragons, The Unofficial Beetlejuice! Beetlejuice! Beetlejuice! Cookbook* and *Cooking for Wizards, Warriors and Dragons*. The editor and Hugo Award-winning cofounder of *The Book Smugglers* (a science fiction and fantasy book review blog), Thea is a hapa (half) Filipina-American who was born in Hawaii and grew up in Indonesia and Japan before moving to the United States. She is a full-time book nerd who works in publishing and currently resides in Marlboro, New York, with her husband and their rambunctious cat.

PAMELA WIZNITZER is an award-winning mixologist based in New York City and has worked around the world bringing cocktail culture to life. She was named one of *Food & Wine* magazine's top 10 Rising Star Mixologists, was an inductee into the Dame Hall of Fame in 2015 and is one of *Wine Enthusiast* magazine's "40 Under 40" (now "Future 40"). She has been featured in multiple publications including *The New York Times, The Wall Street Journal, Zagat, Glamour, Bloomberg* and *Esquire* and makes recurring media appearances on the the Food Network, VH1 and NBC. You can find more of her recipes and cocktail inspiration by following her on Instagram: *@pamwiz*.

Media Lab Books
For inquiries, call 646-449-8614

Copyright © 2023 by Topix Media Lab

Published by Topix Media Lab
14 Wall Street, Suite 3C
New York, NY 10005

Printed in China

ISBN-13: 978-1-956403-43-5
ISBN-10: 1-956403-43-4

CEO Tony Romando

Vice President & Publisher Phil Sexton
Senior Vice President of Sales & New Markets Tom Mifsud
Vice President of Retail Sales & Logistics Linda Greenblatt
Chief Financial Officer Vandana Patel
Manufacturing Director Nancy Puskuldjian
Digital Marketing & Strategy Manager Elyse Gregov

Chief Content Officer Jeff Ashworth
Director of Editorial Operations Courtney Kerrigan
Senior Acquisitions Editor Noreen Henson
Creative Director Susan Dazzo
Photo Director Dave Weiss
Executive Editor Tim Baker
Managing Editor Tara Sherman

Content Editor Juliana Sharaf
Content Designer Mikio Sakai
Features Editor Trevor Courneen
Designer Glen Karpowich
Copy Editor & Fact Checker Madeline Raynor
Junior Designer Alyssa Bredin Quirós
Assistant Photo Editor Jenna Addesso

Additional art: Shutterstock

Indexing by R studio T, NYC